Henry Heavisides

The Minstrelsy of Britain

Or, a glance at our lyrical poetry and poets, from the reign of Queen

Elizabeth to the present time, including a dissertation on the genius and

lyrics of Burns

Henry Heavisides

The Minstrelsy of Britain
*Or, a glance at our lyrical poetry and poets, from the reign of Queen Elizabeth to
the present time, including a dissertation on the genius and lyrics of Burns*

ISBN/EAN: 9783744774888

Printed in Europe, USA, Canada, Australia, Japan

Cover: Foto ©Thomas Meinert / pixelio.de

More available books at **www.hansebooks.com**

THE MINSTRELSY OF BRITAIN.

THE
MINSTRELSY OF BRITAIN;

OR A GLANCE AT

Our Lyrical Poetry and Poets

FROM THE

REIGN OF QUEEN ELIZABETH TO THE PRESENT TIME,

INCLUDING A

DISSERTATION

ON THE

GENIUS AND LYRICS OF BURNS.

BY HENRY HEAVISIDES,
Author of the " Pleasures of Home."

STOCKTON:
PRINTED BY HENRY HEAVISIDES.

1860.

TO

JOHN REED APPLETON, F. S. A.,

WESTERN HILL, DURHAM,

THIS VOLUME

Is Dedicated,

WITH THE WARMEST FEELINGS OF ESTEEM,

BY HIS SINCERE FRIEND,

THE AUTHOR.

PREFACE.

THE greater portion of the contents of this work was delivered some time since by the author in the form of lectures—and though he then stood in a new position as a public lecturer, yet he is proud to say, that they were listened to with marked attention by large auditories. Having frequently been solicited to publish the lectures, he has lately re-written them, with the addition of much new matter; and now, more suitably arranged for publication, he respectfully presents the produce of his efforts to the public, humbly hoping that the volume will be found worthy of perusal—and, in many respects, an appropriate companion to the third edition of his " Pleasures of Home."

Stockton, Aug. 3rd, 1860.

CONTENTS.

OUR LYRICAL POETRY AND POETS.

CHAPTER VI.

———

THE GENIUS AND LYRICS OF BURNS.

CHAPTER VII.

CHAPTER VIII.

CHAPTER IX.

CHAPTER X.

CHAPTER XI.

CHAPTER XII.

Our Lyrical Poetry and Poets.

CHAPTER I.

The power of Lyrical poetry—the Elizabethan age—
Shakspere, Carew, Jonson, &c.

It is generally acknowledged by those best acquainted with the subject, that Lyrical Poetry has
more power over the human heart than any other
species of poetical literature. The lyre had its origin
in remote ages, when the bards or minstrels of old,
by the light of their own inspiration, sang of passing
events or the heroic achievements of warriors, and
thus, at the same time, gave birth both to Poetry and
Music.

At a more advanced period, when "burning Sappho loved and sung," and when Pindar and Anacreon
composed their inimitable odes, such effusions were
generally sung and accompanied by the lyre, a musical instrument much in vogue at that time in Greece,
and from the name of which instrument the poetry now
denominated Lyrical owes its present appellation.
Since that distant age our lyrical literature has been
enriched by the best poets with the sweetest poetic
strains, so pure in diction, so just in sentiment, and

so truthful to Nature that outliving even the pyra-
mids and the most enduring marble monuments they
will be valued and admired as long as there are human hearts to feel their power and appreciate their
beauty.

The Lyric is undoubtedly the purest and highest
order of Poetry.   It requires the most exalted genius
to excel in it.   While the productions of the Epic
Muse have sprung into existence and soon been no
more, we see the rich parterre of her lyric sister still
glowing with the choicest flowers of Poesy, blooming
in perennial beauty, ever fresh and ever fair! How
are we to account for this? The reason is obvious.
The effusions of the latter Muse speak to the heart in
the simple language of Truth and with all the force
of musical expression. When energetic, how trumpet
tongued are her strains—when plaintive, how touching and tender—and when, like a seraph from heaven,
she strikes her divine harp to Love, how beautiful,
how exquisitely she gives utterance to " thoughts that
breathe and words that burn !"

One of our most popular writers, when speaking
on this subject, says, " The world must become pro-
saic indeed, our railways, our other mechanical triumphs, and our political economy, must produce the
worst effects foretold by our darkest prophets before
the genuine lyric—the Song—will lose its hold on
the human heart. It is the genuine offspring of the
heart, and therefore it will never be forgotten."   The
truth of these observations is established by facts that
cannot be well contradicted.   " Give me the making
of the national ballads," said an illustrious statesman,

"and I care not who makes the laws." In this utilitarian age many will think this remark extremely foolish and extravagant. Those who think so, however, are generally apt to consider even the best Poetry as mere nonsense, and all the time dedicated to Music as time idly wasted, and which might be better and more profitably spent. But those who have paid more attention to this subject—who have deeply felt in their hearts the potent, inexpressible power of "immortal verse married to immortal song"—those who have deeply felt this power, will at once acknowledge there is more justness, more wisdom, and more truth in the emphatic words just quoted than some are aware of or others are disposed to admit.

Innumerable instances, both from ancient and modern history, might here be cited to prove what we have advanced; but two or three of a modern date must suffice. It is a well-known fact, that the bands of the Swiss regiments were strictly forbidden to play the "Ranz des Vasches," as this national air brought to their recollection the happy scenes of Home, with all its endearing associations, and thus with a strong impulse they wished to return to their native country. What, during the latter part of the last century, so much contributed to hurl the Bourbons from the throne of France? The Marseilles Hymn. What greatly accelerated in that kingdom the downfall of the unfortunate Louis Philip? The spirit of Liberty burning in that hymn like a volcanic fire. What contributed to quell the mutiny of the Nore, and induced our disaffected seamen to return to a state of subordination? The naval songs of Dib-

din, which so powerfully tended, during our war with
France, to rouse our "ocean warriors" to the highest pitch of patriotic daring and enthusiasm. Inspired
too by the shrill tones of the bagpipe how frequently
have our highland regiments fought and conquered.
And as one of our writers has said, "Who knows
how much of loyalty might have remained unexcited
if the music of the national anthem had not been so
magnificent, and the air of "Rule Britannia" had
had not been so inspiriting?"

Such is the power of the Lyric, which is certainly
the most delightful species of our poetic literature.
But the Lyric Muse instructs as well as delights. In
the most captivating style she brings before us the
pure and the beautiful, both in the natural and the
moral world.   Alike in the lowly cot and the stately
hall—alike in the home circle as at the social
board—she brings "to our business and bosoms"
thoughts and feelings "too deep for tears." Where-
ever we move and have our being she displays to us
all the realities of life, and thus shews us "the image
of man and of nature," which is the *very essence*,
the *very soul* of Poetry, emphatically denominated
by Wordsworth, as the first and last of all knowledge,
as it is the language of the heart.

We shall now dismiss this part of our subject and
proceed to give a passing glance at the productions
of our most popular lyrists from the reign of Queen
Elizabeth to the present time, and in doing this we
shall endeavour to shew the wide difference that exists
between a pure and a vitiated taste for metrical compositions, especially such as have been set to music.

The reign of Elizabeth has justly been termed the golden age of English poetic literature, for it was the age of Shakespeare, the great exponent of human nature, the intellectual Titan, who "piles up his magnificent thoughts, Olympus high, grasps the lightnings of creative Jove, and speaks the words that call spirits and mortals and worlds into existence." It was the age of Beaumont and Fletcher, the Siamese twins in dramatic literature, whose lyrics are so sweet in versification and so highly polished that even at the present day they might pass for modern productions. It was the age of Massinger, and Spencer, and Jonson—"O rare Ben Jonson"—the minor poets at that period being George Wither, Drummond, Browne, Carew, Herrick, and others, whose lyrics for elegance of diction and originality of thought can scarcely be surpassed. These were the mighty master spirits of that glorious age, who formed the brightest galaxy of poetic genius that ever shed lustre on the literary hemisphere. "They being dead yet speaketh." Though their mortal remains have long laid mouldering in the tomb, yet their words, their thoughts, stamped with the impress of immortality, will live and breathe to the "last syllable of recorded Time."

The lyrics of Shakespeare are still sung in his unrivalled dramatic works, the music to Macbeth being composed by John Locke, who flourished in the 17th century, and the music to the songs in the "Tempest" and "As you like it," being the joint production of Dr. Bull and Dr. Arne, who lived in the same age.

That some idea may be formed of the sweet songs

of the Elizabethan era, we shall now give two specimens of them, our limits not allowing us to give
more. The first, as follows, is by Thomas Carew :—

> " He that loves a rosy cheek,
>   Or a coral lip admires,
> Or from starlike eyes doth seek
>   Fuel to maintain its fires,
> As old Time makes these decay
> So his flames must waste away.
>
> But a smooth and stedfast mind,
>   Gentle thoughts and calm desires,
> Hearts with equal love combined
>   Kindle never-dying fires ; .
> Where these are not, I despise
> Lovely cheeks, or lips, or eyes."

The next specimen is the song entitled " Drink to
me only with thine eyes." This song is from the
pen of Ben Jonson. It has long floated on the stream
of popularity, and still continues a favorite in the
musical world.

Illustration.

DRINK TO ME ONLY WITH THINE EYES.

> Drink to me only with thine eyes
>   And I will pledge with mine,
> Or leave a kiss but in the cup
>   And I'll not look for wine.
> The thirst that from my soul doth rise
>   Doth ask a drink divine,
> But might I of Jove's nectar sup
>   I would not change for thine.
>
> I sent thee late a rosy wreath
>   Not so much honouring thee
> As giving it a hope, that there
>   It would not withered be ;

But thou thereon didst only breathe,
   And sent it back to me ;
Since then it grows and smells, I swear,
   Not of itself but thee.

This song and the one previously quoted were composed nearly 300 years ago, yet how musically, how sweetly they flow! They will bear comparison with the best songs of the present day, and present a refreshing contrast to the numberless insipid compositions which have lately been set to music.

It is not known who is the composer of the beautiful air adapted to the last song, " Drink to me only with thine eyes." It must have been composed, however, many years after the reign of Elizabeth, as it is said there is not a scrap now extant of the original music to the lyrics of that period.

CHAPTER II.

*Reign of Charles II.—a decline in literary taste—
the Commonwealth—Milton and Dryden.*

Though rather tinctured with a quaintness of expression peculiar to that age, yet the lyrical poetry of the Elizabethan era, was so extremely original in thought and so truthful in feeling, uniting Doric simplicity with vigour of diction, that the songs then composed might have stood as models for future lyrists. But not so :—a decline in literary taste began in the reign of Charles the second, and the taste for such sweet compositions as those of Carew, Browne,

Suckling, Herrick, and others, was at once superseded
by a strange and unnatural mania for Pastoral Love
ditties and Bacchanalian drinking songs. The in-
sipidity of the one could only be equalled by the vulgarity of the other.   In the amatory effusions just
alluded to there is no truth, no nature, no genuine
feeling.   A perusal of them leads one to imagine, that
in by-gone days the length and breadth of old England
was swarming with love-sick shepherds and shepherdesses, who, like amorous turtle doves, had nothing
else to do but bill and coo amid arcadian scenes
where   murmuring   streams   eternally   meandered
through flowery meeds and myrtle groves.

A writer on this subject says, that "Corydon then
wept among his flocks because Chloe or Phœbe was
cruel, and Chole called upon echo to repeat the name
of Corydon, the falsest of shepherds and of men."
O hopeless, unrequited Love! thou relentless breaker
of human hearts! were all true that babbling poets
tell us of the shepherdesses of that puling age, how
terrible must be thy power!

We have now in our possession upwards of one
hundred songs, set to music, which were highly popular in the middle of the last century.   We shall
make two or three extracts from them merely to shew
the depraved taste for ballad writing at that period.
The first song to which we call attention is entitled
"The Shepherd's Complaint," and it concludes thus:

  " To Nanny's poultry oats I gave,
   I'm sure I always had the best,
  Within this week her pigeons have
   Eat *up a peck of peas at least;*

Her little pigeons kiss, but she
Would never take a kiss from me.

Must Robin always Nanny woo,
    And Nanny still on Robin frown?
Alas! poor wretch, what shall I do
    If Nanny does not love me soon?
If no relief to me she'll bring
I'll hang me in her apron string."

The next song, called "The Despairing Shepherd,"
represents a love-lorn swain bewailing his hard fate
to his brother shepherds circled round him. In tears
he informs them that his cruel Chloe has deserted
him for another, and then he sighs and sighs again,
while his brother shepherds in sympathetic concert,
return sigh for sigh, till at last he ceases his melancholy plaint in the following words:—

" But, oh! one more deserving
    Has thaw'd her frozen breast,
Her heart to him devoting
    She's cold to all the rest.
Their love with joy abounding,
    The thought disturbs my brain,
O cruel maid, then *swooning*,
    He fell upon the plain!"

Alas, poor shepherd! the bare recital of his woes
was too much for him, so he swooned, and fell upon
the plain, a victim, no doubt, to unrequited love.

Another despairing swain in a situation similar to
the last, after complaining of his Celia's cruelty, thus
ends his piteous plaint:—

" But Celia, when this conquest's won,
    And *I am gone and cold ;*
Renounce the cruel deed you've done,
    Nor glory when 'tis told ;
For every lovely generous maid
    Will *take my injured part,*
And *curse thee,* Celia, I'm afraid,
    For *breaking my poor heart!*"

These extracts sufficiently shew the character of
the lack-a-daisical love effusions, which, with a host of
vile Bacchanalian songs, equally as silly, were quite
the rage for nearly two centuries, and were certainly
a disgrace to the literature of that period. The fact
is, the race of lyrists by whom they were composed
sang not from their hearts. They sang of Love indeed,
but not with the passionate warmth and truth of
Sappho and Petrarch—they sang in praise of wine,
but not with the elegance and sparkling wit of
Anacreon, and therefore it is matter of astonishment,
at the present day, how productions so vapid could
have retained so long a hold on the public mind.

In comparison with the silly effusions we have
just alluded to, how full of purity and truthfulness
and beauty appears the following pastoral production,
by Cunningham, a sweet pastoral poet and comedian,
who played several seasons at the Stockton theatre,
and who died at Newcastle during the latter part of
the last century.

Illustration.

WHEN THE ROSY MORN APPEARING.

When the rosy morn appearing
  Paints with gold the verdant lawn,
Bees, on banks of thyme disporting,
  Sip the sweets and hail the dawn.

Warbling birds, the day proclaiming,
  Carol sweet the lively strain,
They forsake their leafy dwelling
  To secure the golden grain.

See, content, the humble gleaner,
  Take the scatter'd ears that fall,
Nature, all her children viewing,
  Kindly bounteous cares for all.

———

The music to these verses was composed by Shield. It is considered extremely beautiful, and when sung by the reapers in the opening scene of the opera of Rosina, where it is introduced, a more pleasing picture of rustic felicity cannot be imagined. Shield was born near North Shields, and though apprenticed to a boat-builder at that place, he afterwards rose by his musical genius to be the finest and most original composer, except Purcell, that this country ever produced. Most of the songs connected with his imperishable music are still sung and much appreciated.

We return now to the drinking songs of the last century, to which we have previously alluded. It is

pleasing to remark, that the taste for songs of this description has been gradually declining for some time
past.   This speaks well for the growing intelligence
of the age, as such songs are generally of a senseless
description, and have a strong tendency to debase the
man.

A sensible writer, Hugh Kelly, says, in a work
published some years ago, " There is nothing at
which I am more offended than the unpardonable
vein of ignorance and brutality so generally introduced in our drinking songs; nor any thing, in my
opinion, which shews a greater reflection upon the
understanding of a sensible society."   It has justly
been observed by another writer, that " every nation
in proportion as it is civilized has abolished intem-
perance in wine, and consequently must be bar-
barous as it is addicted to excess.   We are apt to
place good fellowship in riot; and have but too
natural a promptitude in imagining that the happiness of an evening is promoted by an extravagant
circulation of the glass; hence are the songs of festi-
vity fraught with continual encomiums on the pleasure of intoxication, and the whole tribe of Bacchanalian lyrics telling us how wonderfully sensible it is
to destroy our senses, and that nothing can be more
rational in a human creature than to drink till he
has not left himself *a glimmer of reason* at all."

As we have given two or three extracts from Pastoral Love Songs we shall now quote from two
Bacchanalian songs, which may be considered as fair
specimens of the rest.   The first, entitled " Fill each

Bowl," begins with the following strange and ludicrous stanza :—

> " Fill each bowl with flowing measure,
>   Till it sparkles o'er the brim,
>   The grave of Care and spring of Pleasure
>   Is *when the brains in nectar swim.*"

We are here told that the spring of Pleasure is
" when the brains in nectar swim!" What a beautiful idea for a poet! The other song we shall quote
from was long a favorite with the votaries of Bacchus.
The former is entitled "Fill each bowl," but the
title of this is, "Fill me a bowl." It is rather odd,
but so it is, that most of our drinking songs com-
mence with filling the bowl, which is generally the
first idea they develop. The following is the first
verse of the song alluded to :—

> " Fill me a bowl—a mighty bowl—
>   Large as my capacious soul—
>   *Vast* as my *thirst* is, let it have
>   *Depth* enough to be my *grave!*
>   I mean the grave of all my care,
>   For I design to bury't there."

It would be idle to criticise this verse—but the
song with which it commences may be considered as a
true representative of most of our drinking songs,
which, in general, express only two ideas. The first,
which is the most important, is to fill the bowl to the
brim, and the other, as a matter of course, is to drink
and drown all care and sorrow, and he that is the
the first to fall, why, " Down among the dead men
let him lie."

A refrain to one of the popular drinking songs of the last century runs thus :—

> " And this is law I will maintain
>   Till wine shall *wash me away*, Sir,
> That whatsoever king shall reign
>   I'll drink my *gallon a day*, Sir."

By this refrain we may imagine that in the last century both loyalty and drinking were in the ascendant, as the measure of a man's loyalty then seems to have been one gallon of wine per day, no matter what king reigned.

Though the period of which we have been speaking shewed so much depravity in the national taste for metrical compositions, yet about that time an immortal bard arose, whose " soul was like a star, and dwelt apart," and whose exalted genius shed a new and radiant light on our poetic literature. We allude to Milton, who has no superior save Shakspere, and whose lyrics are considered the best in our language. Alike musician and poet, with a mind irradiated by beatific visions, the nicety of his ear is evident in all his works, especially in the masque of Comus and some of his minor productions, which breathe the very soul of harmony.

Soon after Milton struck his divine harp another luminary burst upon the literary world. This bright star was Dryden, "glorious John Dryden," whose vigorous verse flows from the " well of English undefiled," and whose St. Cecilia and Alexander's Feast are of themselves sufficient to hand down his name to future generations. With their transcendant genius, however, it is said that neither of these distinguished poets experienced happiness in the conjugal state. It is recorded that Dryden very much disliked his wife, and that one day while in his study, poring over his manuscripts, she happened to enter. The poet taking no notice of her, she naturally felt piqued, and said to him, " I wish I were a book and then you would pay me more attention." Dryden immediately answered, " I would like you then to be an almanack, and then I could change you at the end of the year."

Though Milton and Dryden both flourished during the Commonwealth, a period when ascetic puritanism endeavoured to nip every blossom of Poesy in the bud ; yet some of the songs they then introduced, set to music by Purcell and Arne, have survived two centuries, and are still occasionally sung and admired in circles were a taste prevails for enjoying, to use a beautiful idea of Tennyson's, " perfect music linked to noble words."

Dryden died in 1701, and from his songs we select the following :—

Illustration.

FAIR, SWEET, AND YOUNG.

Fair, sweet, and young, receive a prize
Reserv'd for your victorious eyes :
From crowds, whom at your feet you see,
Oh, pity and distinguish me !
As I from thousand beauties more
Distinguish you, and only you adore.

Your face for conquest was design'd ;
Your every motion charms my mind ;
Angels, when you your silence break,
Forget their hymns to hear you speak ;
But when at once they hear and view,
Are loth to mount, and long to stay with you.

No graces can your form improve,
But all are lost unless you love ;
While that sweet passion you disdain,
Your veil and beauty are in vain :
In pity then prevent my fate,
For after dying all reprieve's too late.

The music to this song is by Purcell, who is styled
the father of our national Ballad music.   One of our
writers in praise of this eminent composer, states,
that "during the brief span of his existence, which
extended only to seven and thirty years, he produced
a large body of dramatic music, which remains to
this day unrivalled in England, and not surpassed in
any other country."   It is rather remarkable that
Bellini, Burns, Byron, Raffaelle, and many other
gifted individuals died at the age of thirty-seven—
an age which has always been considered extremely
fatal to the gifted possessors of exalted genius.

CHAPTER III.

The reigns of William III, Queen Anne, and George 1st—Pope, Gay, Gray, Collins, Allan Ramsay, and Lady Anne Barnard.

The period comprising the reigns of William III, Queen Anne, and George I. has been termed the Augustan era of English literature. This period was distinguished for the wits and poets that then shed so bright a lustre on the republic of letters. At the head of these poets stood Alexander Pope, whose biting satire and didactic verse display the vigour of his poetic genius. Like Swift, however, his contemporary, he possessed neither the Doric simplicity nor the magnificent imagination necessary for the composition of the true lyric. The only one in the circle of wits and poets at that time pre-eminently gifted as a lyrical writer, and in any way calculated to excel as one, was Gay,

> " Of manners gentle, of affections mild,
> In wit a man, simplicity a child."

This poet was the first that attempted to improve the then prevalent taste for mock affectation in Love pastorals. He wrote a large number of songs; but the whole of them have sunk into oblivion, except the lively effusion of " Cease your Funning," the pathetic ballad of " Black-eyed Susan," and a few more

D

pieces possessing similar poetic merit, and which still retain their position as admirable English ballads both as regards the words and the music.

Illustration.

BLACK-EYED SUSAN.

All in the Downs the fleet was moor'd,
 The streamers waving in the wind,
When black-eyed Susan came on board,
 O where shall I my true love find ?
Tell me, ye jovial sailors, tell me true,
If my sweet William sails among your crew ?

William, who high upon the yard,
 Rock'd by the billows to and fro,
Soon as the well-known voice he heard,
 He sighed and cast his eyes below.
The cord flew swiftly through his glowing hands,
And quick as lightning on the deck he stands.

" O Susan, Susan, lovely dear,
 My vows shall always true remain,
Let me kiss off that falling tear,
 We only part to meet again ;   .
Change as ye list, ye winds, my heart shall be
The faithful compass that still points to thee.

Believe not what the landsmen say,
 Who tempt with doubts thy constant mind ;
They tell thee sailors, when away,
 In every port a mistress find ;
Yes, yes, believe them when they tell thee so,
For thou art present wheresoe'er I go."

The boatswain gave the dreadful word,
   The sails their swelling bosom spread;
No longer she must stay on board,—
   They kiss'd, she sighed, he hung his head:
Her lessening boat unwilling rows to land,
" Adieu!" she cried, and waved her lily hand.

———

The music to this ballad is beautiful. It was
arranged by Leveridge, from an old English melody.
The late Douglas Jerrold, no doubt, was indebted to
this song for the idea of his popular drama of " Black-
eyed Susan," which so much contributed to establish
his fame as a dramatic writer.

In taking a hasty glance at the lyrists of Britain
since the Elizabethan era we cannot pass unnoticed
those highly-gifted poets, Gray and Collins. Neither
of these favorite sons of Apollo wrote much, but the
little they did write was written well. By their incom-
parable odes they have obtained permanent niches in
the temple of Fame, and abounding as these odes do,
with natural sentiments and splendid imagery, clothed
in all the elegance of classical language, they can
never fail to charm those who have a taste for lyrical
compositions of the highest order.

With none of the sublimity and lofty imagination
so conspicuous in the odes of Gray and Collins; but
in strains simple, yet touching and truthful, the old
Scotch bard, Allan Ramsay, about this period, attuned
his harp to sing of rural life and scenes. As a true
and faithful delineator of Scottish manners in humble life he has no superior. His effusions contain

none of those forced conceits and puling sentimentality
which disgraced most of the ballads then produced.
His shepherds and shepherdesses, therefore, are not
described as love-sick creatures whimpering, and
whining, and sighing, and howling, amid Arcadian
scenes that never had existence; but, Shakspere-like,
he paints nature with the pencil of Truth, and thus,
warm and genuine from the heart, his characters
invariably develop, with poetic beauty, the natural and
unaffected feelings of the human breast. His "Gentle
Shepherd" is allowed to be the finest pastoral drama
in the world, and as a lyrist, the forerunner of Mac-
neil, Ferguson, Burns, and Tannahill, he may justly
be considered the father of Scottish song, and the
founder of that general taste for ballad poetry in
Scotland which has so long characterised that country.

About the year 1771, two of the most beautiful
ballads ever composed made their appearance. These
sterling productions are the "Flowers of the Forest"
and "Auld Robin Gray." The former effusion, bewailing the losses sustained by the Scotch at the battle of Flodden, was composed by Miss Jane Elliott,
sister to Sir Gilbert Elliott, of Minto, and the authoress
of the latter is Lady Anne Barnard, who set it to an old
Scotch air, so plaintive and so touching, that it is
hard to say, whether the music or the verses possess
the greatest beauty.

It is rather singular that the fair composer of this
charming ballad kept the authorship of it a profound
secret for the long space of fifty years. In 1823, however, only two years before her death, she acknow-

ledged the composition of it in a letter to Sir Walter
Scott.

The ballad of "Auld Robin Gray" displays
much genuine feeling and extreme tenderness, expressed in language so natural and appropriate, that
it will ever retain its position in the musical world as
a very superior production.

How beautifully this effusion commences with the
following verse :—

" When the sheep are in the fauld and a' the kye at hame,
And a' the weary world to sleep are gane,
The waes o' my heart fall in showers from my e'e,
While my gude man sleeps sound by me."

And then when it is told that the father of " Jennie"
" could nae wark," and her " mither could nae spin,"
and for the sake of getting a livelihood they both endeavour to prevail upon her to marry " Auld Rob,"
how happily conceived is the following couplet :—

" My faither urged me sair, my mither did nae speak,
But she look'd in my face till my heart was like to break !"

Nothing can be more natural and touching than
the last line of this couplet. But every verse of
this sweet composition contains sentiments, though
simply expressed, which are full of poetic feeling and
beauty.

CHAPTER IV.

The age of Dibdin—his patriotic and sea songs—the effect they had on our seamen—Burns, his wonderful powers as a lyrist.

It has previously been remarked, that the perverted taste for Pastoral love ditties began to be prevalent so far back as the reign of Charles II. This taste, strange to say, continued, more or less, until the latter part of the last century, when it gradually declined as the naval and other songs of Charles Dibdin became popular.

Though this prolific song writer was the author of much trash, yet his best compositions shew that he was not deficient either in poetic or musical genius. His songs amount to 1260 in number. The most popular of them, no doubt, owed much of their extraordinary popularity to the strong patriotic feeling that existed in every British bosom during the threatened invasion of this country by Napoleon I. Produced at this memorable period, they mostly eulogised the dauntless heroism of our British tars, or contained threats to give the French a good drubbing if they dared to land upon our coast. These sentiments were congenial then to the warlike feelings of John Bull, who, at that time, firmly believed in his own heart that one Englishman, fed on roast beef, was more than a match for five Frenchmen living on frog soup.

Dibdin is generally acknowledged as a clever writer; but, we must say, that a great number of his effusions cannot but be considered as pernicious in their tendency. They abound with false sentiments which inculcate improvident and intemperate habits in the British sailor, and thus urge him to squander away his money, to be reckless, and thoughtless, and "laughing in Care's face," to drink grog as the summit of all earthly enjoyments.

To shew the very extravagant extent to which the drinking songs at that period went the following laughable effusion of Dibdin's in praise of grog is presented:—

——

Illustration.

THERE'S NOTHING LIKE GROG.

A plague on these musty old lubbers
 Who tell us to fast and to think,
And patient fall in with life's rubbers
 With nothing but water to drink;
A can of good stuff had they swigged it
 'Twould have set them for pleasure agog,
  And in spite of the rules
  Of the schools
  The old fools
Would all of them swigged it,
And swore there was nothing like grog.

My father when last I from Guinea
 Returned with abundance of wealth,
Cried, " Jack, never be such a ninny
 To drink"—said I, " Father, your health!"

So I shew'd him the stuff and he twigged it,
  And it set the old codger agog,
    And he swigged it and mother,
    And sister and brother,
And I swigged and all of us swigged it,
And swore there was nothing like grog.

'Tother day as the chaplain was preaching,
  Behind him I cautiously slunk,
And while he our duty was teaching,
  As how we should never get drunk,
I shew'd him the stuff and he twigged it,
  And it soon set his reverence agog,
    And he swigged and Dick swigged,
    And Ben swigg'd and Nick swigged,
And I swigged, and all of us swigged it,
And swore there was nothing like grog.

———

This song, it must be allowed, is the very antithesis to the principles of the Temperance movement. In praise of drinking it goes the *whole hog.* Many of Dibdin's songs, however, contain passages of a redeeming character—passages possessing great poetic merit, that not only inculcate the highest sentiments of generosity and humanity, but strongly instill the patriotic principle that " England expects every man to do his duty."

Dibdin, speaking of his own songs, says, " they have been considered an object of national consequence ; they have been the solace of sailors in long passages, in storm, and in battle ; and have been quoted in mutinies to the restoration of order and discipline."

Indeed, they were considered of so much national consequence in fanning the flame of patriotism during our war with France that the government granted Dibdin for his services an annual pension for life. When the whigs, however, came into office in 1814, this pension was taken off, and poor Dibdin, grown old and infirm, was suffered to breathe his last, neglected and forgotten, in the greatest destitution and distress. Such, alas, is too often the fate of genius!

In the age of Dibdin, though gifted with a far superior genius to him, appeared the inspired ploughman, Robert Burns, "who walked in glory by the mountain's side." Like Shakspere, he too was the poet of nature; and though but a ploughman, isolated as it were from men of letters, and mixing only with the peasantry of his native vale; yet, by the power of his own magnificent genius, he rose to be one of the brightest ornaments to imaginative literature. In exquisite tenderness, impassioned feeling, or the outpourings of a noble and an independent spirit, where is the poet that can surpass him? Whatever he touched he beautified, enhanced by the happiest and most felicitous expression. Looking at Nature with a poet's eye as he wandered among the "birks and braes" so dear to him, he caught inspiration from the material imagery around him, and in strains melodious and truthful he sang from the depths of his own sensitive heart. His principal lyrics, especially his songs, abound with numberless beauties. To point out one as superior in poetic excellence to others would be a difficult task. Where all is beautiful it seems im-

E

possible to select. A rich parterre may present to
us the choicest flowers, all having particular claims
to our admiration. Sweetly intermingled with the
blushing rose we may behold the graceful pink, the
fragrant wall-flower, the modest violet, and other
productions of Flora; but though all appear lovely,
yet they possess distinctive hues, distinctive fragrance,
and distinctive varieties; therefore to cull one as a
representative of the rest would be utterly impossible.
So it is with the best songs of Burns. They all
appear beautiful; but when minutely examined, we
find that each contains some distinct poetic beauty,
some fascinating charm, diversified by some distinct
shade of deep feeling, so that it is difficult to select
one as superior to the rest. But unlike the flowers
of the parterre, which are doomed soon to wither,
perish, and be no more, the poetic products of
Scotia's best and noblest bard will bloom for ever,
and be admired for their beauty as long as "rivers
roll and vales are green."

Burns wrote 268 songs, 120 of which, written
when his judgment was matured, he composed for
Thomson's splendid edition of Scottish songs. Burns
spurned the idea of being paid for his poetic services
to this work, as, to use his own emphatic words, he
considered it "would be downright prostitution of
soul." Allan Cunningham, speaking of these songs,
says, "It is rather remarkable, that the most naturally
elegant and impassioned songs in our literature were
written by a ploughman." Another eminent writer,
Samuel Tyler, when alluding to them, remarks that

"They were conceived and bodied forth in music. They are the gems of thought floating in streams of music, and there are in Scotland few firesides where they are not sung every evening, diffusing through the hearth the sweetness of spiritual pleasure, and refining the sensibilities, by the purifying sympathy with generous sentiments."

Burns composed most of his lyrics in the open air as he mused on surrounding objects. His well-known effusion, "Ye banks and braes of bonnie Doon," exemplifies the truth of this remark. In the moment of inspiration, when about to compose this song, we may imagine him musing in loneliness on the banks of the Doon when all Nature was redolent with beauty. He gazes on the scene, but his heart is sad. It is not in unison with the joyousness around him. He, therefore, with a turn of thought peculiar to himself, thus gives utterance to his feelings :—

> " Ye banks and braes o' bonnie Doon
>   How can ye bloom sae fresh and fair ;
> How can ye chant, ye little birds,
>   And I sae weary, fu' o' care?"

One of these feathered choristers then attracts his notice, and how sweet, how tender is the strain he continues,

> " Thou'lt break my heart, thou warbling bird,
>   That wantons thro' the flowering thorn ;
> Thou minds me o' departed joys,
>   Departed—never to return."

The air adapted to this song was the composition of an amateur of Edinbro'. Napoleon Bonaparte, when conversing with a lady at St. Helena, said, it was the only *English* air that he could endure. All our other airs he considered execrable. It would have been better for the hero of Marengo if he had never made a more egregious mistake.

—

Illustration.

YE BANKS AND BRAES O' BONNIE DOON.

Ye banks and braes o' bonnie Doon,
 How can ye bloom sac fresh and fair ;
How can ye chant, ye little birds,
 And I sae weary, fu' o' care !
Thou'lt break my heart, thou warbling bird,
 That wantons thro' the flowering thorn,
Thou minds me o' departed joys,
 Departed—never to return.

Aft hae I rov'd by bonnie Doon,
 To see the rose and woodbine twine ;
While ilka bird sang o' its luve,
 And fondly sae did I o' mine.
Wi' heartsome glee I pu'd a rose,
 Fu' sweet upon its thorny tree :
And my fause luver stole my rose,
 But, ah ! he left the thorn wi' me

CHAPTER V.

*The beginning of the 19th century—the galaxy of
poets then—anecdotes of Campbell—the lyrics of
Eliza Cooke and Mackay.*

The most remarkable period in the history of
Literature and Science, perhaps, ever known, is
from the commencement of the 19th century to the
present time. For though the astonishing achievements of Science during this period have been such
as to give us, in appearance, a strong utilitarian character; yet, it must be admitted, we think, that the
progress of poetic literature has kept pace with our
mechanical triumphs. The last half century is distinguished, like the Elizabethan era, for the long
list of noble poets who adorned it; at the head of
whom may be noticed Wordsworth, Coleridge, Southey,
Byron, Keats, Shelley, Sir Walter Scott, and Campbell, who, in every diversified form, have enriched
our literature with the brightest gems of Poesy.

But where are now those refulgent stars that once
excited our admiration and shed a blaze of glory over
the poetic firmament? One by one they have disap-
peared from amongst us—one by one they have
passed "that awful bourne none e'er repassed,"
and their disappearance has left a blank in the literary world that has not yet been supplied.

The poems of these bards are undoubtedly of the

highest order ; but Wordsworth, Byron, Scott, and
Campbell, in this galaxy of genius, can only be considered as lyrical writers.   Many of Scott's songs are
spirited compositions, which sustain their deserved
popularity.   The songs by Byron are few, but worthy of his genius.   Those by Campbell do not com-
prise thirty in number, but they can scarcely be ex-
celled for vigour and beauty.   His martial songs are
the most magnificent effusions in our language.   They
glow with heroic thoughts expressed with the " eloquence of Truth."   Every strain is manly and impassioned, every line energetic, sounding like a trumpet-
blast on the battle field.   Campbell is the bard of
modern Chivalry, the William Tell of patriotic lyrists,
who gives utterance to sentiments which are enshrined in every bosom animated with a love of
Freedom.   No poet evinces so strong, so utter a detes-
tation of Slavery and all despotic rulers as Campbell.
He bids defiance to them in words of fire.   With a
race of poets like him what country wearing a tyrant's
fetters would not rise and burst them ?   How spirited
are the following lines from his " Song to the Greeks"
when he calls upon them to " burst the tyrant's
chain," and prove themselves " heroes descended from
heroes" :—

" Again to the battle, Achaians,
   Our hearts bid the tyrants defiance ;
   Our land, the first garden of Liberty's tree—
   It has been, and shall yet be, the land of the free.
   A breath of submission we breathe not,
   The sword that we've drawn we will sheathe not !

Its scabbard is left where our martyrs are laid,
And the vengeance of ages has whetted its blade.
Earth may hide—waves engulf—fire consume us,
But they shall not to slavery doom us.
Accursed may his memory blacken
If a coward there be who would slacken
Till we've trampled the turban, and shown ourselves
    worth
Being sprung from and named for the godlike of earth.
Strike home, and the world shall revere us,
As heroes descended from heroes."

It is rather remarkable that Campbell, though a most acute critic of the poetry of others, should want the necessary judgment to form a correct estimate of his own. Several of our greatest poets were alike faulty in this respect. Milton always thought his "Paradise Regained" far superior to his "Paradise Lost;" but no one ever thought so but himself. Thomson, the gifted author of the "Seasons," considered his long, dry, and prosy poem, "Liberty," as his best production. Campbell, however, not depending on his own judgment, was in the habit of submitting his manuscript poems for approval to his brother, who was an excellent judge of poetry, though no poet. One day Campbell handed to his brother a poem which he had just composed, and requested his opinion of it. His brother having attentively perused the composition shook his head, when Campbell hastily exclaimed, "What is the matter with it? Wont it do? What does it want?" "It wants fire!" replied his brother, and he immediately threw the manuscript into the fire to the great mortification of the poet, who had not another copy.

Campbell, when once in conversation with Sir Walter Scott, said, that "he thought nothing of his 'Hohenlinden'—it was too full of trumpet lines," and strange to say, he never saw the beauties in that immortal ode until pointed out to him then by the author of Waverley. And so it was with his poem, "The Last Man," one of the finest imaginative compositions ever produced. He set little value on this beautiful lyric until he heard it sung by Braham at a concert in Edinbro'. But we shall give, in Campbell's own words, his brief relation of this circumstance. He says, that "During a visit to Edinbro' I was induced to accompany a friend one evening to a concert, where, unexpectedly, I heard my own song, "The Last Man." I shall ever remember my feelings whilst listening. I was overpowered with my own conceptions—*I wept*—and for the first time I felt that I was a poet!"

How simple, yet how touching is this account of Campbell's feelings! He listened to his own song, and overpowered by his conceptions *he wept* and for the first time *felt that he was a poet.* Such is the magic power of song.

Campbell had an annuity of two hundred pounds awarded to him by government soon after the publication of his "Pleasures of Hope," which he produced at twenty-three years of age. He received this annuity as long as he lived. "Few modern poets," says a popular writer, when speaking of Campbell,

" have received a more bountiful harvest of fame and comfort from their labours, and few have proved themselves more worthy of the distinction."

—

Illustration.

THE LAST MAN.

All worldly shapes shall melt in gloom—
  The sun himself must die,
Before this mortal shall assume
  Its immortality !
I saw a vision in my sleep,
That gave my spirit strength to sweep
  Adown the gulf of time !
I saw the last of human mould
That shall creation's death behold,
  As Adam saw her prime !

The sun's eye had a sickly glare,
  The earth with age was wan ;
The skeletons of nations were
  Around that lonely man !
Some had expired in fight—the brands
Still rusted in their bony hands—
  In plague and famine some ;
Earth's cities had no sound or tread,
And ships were drifting with the dead
  To shores where all was dumb !

Yet prophet-like, that lone one stood,
  With dauntless words and high,
That shook the sere leaves from the wood,
  As if a storm passed by ;
Saying, " We are twins in death, proud sun ;
Thy face is cold, thy race is run,

'Tis mercy bids thee go.
For thou, ten thousand thousand years,
Hast seen the tide of human tears,
    That shall no longer flow."

          *   *   *

" This spirit shall return to Him
    That gave its heavenly spark ;
Yet think not, sun, it shall be dim,
    When thou thyself art dark !
No ! it shall live again, and shine
In bliss unknown to beams of thine,
    By him recalled to breath,
Who captive led captivity,
Who robbed the grave of victory,
    And took the sting from death !"

Amongst the popular song-writers at the present
time are Eliza Cook and Charles Mackay, author of
the "*Lump of Gold*." These writers have done much
towards improving the public taste for songs of real
merit, by combining our own characteristic music
with words that tend to elevate our ideas and make
us more in love with the good and the beautiful.

The songs of Eliza Cook, in our opinion, are
highly suitable to effect these objects. They possess
more the truth and vigour of Burns than the elegance
and sparkling fancy of Moore, for like Burns she has
the power of creating the most exalted sentiments
from the commonest objects.   By her own beautiful
thoughts we are told what a " sacred thing" is an old
arm chair.   Her numerous effusions are well calculated to exercise a moral influence upon the minds
of the people, by whom they are much estimated, and
whom by her genius she is eminently qualified to

instruct and elevate though not gifted with great poetic powers.

—

Illustration.

THE OLD ARM CHAIR.

I love it, I love it, and who shall dare
To chide me for loving that old arm chair?
I've treasured it long as a sainted prize,
I've bedewed it with tears, I've embalmed it with sighs;
'Tis bound by a thousand bands to my heart;
Not a tie will break, not a link will start.
Would you know the spell?—a mother sat there!
And a sacred thing is that old arm chair.

In childhood's hour I linger'd near
The hallow'd seat with listening ear;
And gentle words that mother would give
To fit me to die—to teach me to live.
She told me that shame would never betide
With truth for my creed, and God for my guide;
She taught me to lisp my earliest prayer
As I knelt beside that old arm chair.

I sat and watch'd her many a day,
When her eye grew dim, and her locks were grey;
And I almost worshipp'd her when she smil'd,
And turned from the Bible to bless her child.
Years roll'd on, but the last one sped—
My idol was shatter'd, my earth-star fled!
I learnt how much the heart can bear
When I saw her die in her old arm chair.

'Tis past, 'tis past! but I gaze on it now
With quiv'ring breath and throbbing brow :
'Twas there she nursed me, 'twas there she died,
And memory flows with lava tide.
Say it is folly, and deem me weak,
Whilst scalding drops start down my cheek :
But I love it, I love it, and cannot tear
My soul from a mother's old arm chair.

The most prolific song writer of the present day is Charles Mackay, the poet of progress. Though this pleasing writer displays little of the imaginative faculty, though his lyrics are never adorned with the sparking graces of Fancy, yet they are of a healthful and vigorous character. They abound with truthful sentiments, well expressed, that have a powerful tendency to improve the mind and refine the feelings. Many of his songs, such as " *Cheer, boys, cheer,*" and " *There's a good time coming,*" have deservedly gained considerable popularity. He has lately been engaged in composing a series of songs, one hundred in number, for our national music, in which important work he was assisted by the late Sir Henry Bishop, who was so eminently qualified for the undertaking. Such a publication has long been wanted, as it is greatly calculated to enrich our vocal music with strains wherein we may feel

"That magic sympathy of sense with sound
That pictures all it sings."

This work, moreover, has the advantage of preventing

from sinking into oblivion many of our beautiful old English melodies, which, for unaffected simplicity and racy originality, are not surpassed by those of any other country. The object in publishing the songs alluded to, of which the following illustration is a fair specimen, was, we are told, " To restore the music of England to the place in the popular heart which it never would have lost had the morality and graces of the poetry been equal to the beauties of the melodies."

———

Illustration.

THE GREEN LANES OF ENGLAND.

MACKAY.

Through the green lanes of England the long summer day,
We have wander'd at will in our Youth's merry May ;
We snatched at the blooms o'er the hedgerows that hung,
Or mocked the sweet song that the nightingale sung.
    In the Autumn we knew
    Where the blackberries grew,
And the shy hazel nuts hidden deep in the shade,
    Or with shouting and cheer,
    When the Christmas drew near,
In search of the ripe, ruddy holly we stray'd.

But the green lanes of England though dear to us then,
Were dearer by far when we grew to be men,
When the heart's first emotions were fervent and pure,
And the world had no grief that a smile could not cure.
    'Twas beneath the green leaves
    In the calm summer eves,
That we breath'd the young hopes in our bosoms that burn'd ;
    Or in Love's gentle eyes
    Read the tender replies
That shew'd the fond passion as fondly returned.

Ye green lanes of England, wherever we roam,
Ye are link'd in our hearts with the memories of home,
With the sports of our Childhood, the love of our prime,
And the pensive delights of a soberer time.
      Other lands may be fair,
      With their balm-breathing air,
And their beauties and grandeur that charm or appall;
      But to young and to old
      Till our hearts shall grow cold
Shall the green lanes of England be dearer to all.

CHAPTER VI.

The vitiated taste of the present age for Cockney songs—their vulgarity—the negro melodies—the lyrics of Tennyson, Gerald Massey, &c.—Conclusion.

At the present time the depraved taste in this country for songs utterly destitute of the morality and graces noticed in the preceding chapter is a disgrace to the intelligence of the age. Bad as the insipid compositions of the 17th century were, a great number of the songs now popular are still worse. It is really astonishing how such effusions, the very essence of vulgarity, could have become so popular. They are chiefly produced from the Cockney school of versifiers, at the head of which is Sam Cowell, who has obtained a world-wide popularity for singing them. Though entirely devoid of originality, wit, or humour; yet these wretched ditties have been sung in most of the singing saloons and concert rooms in the kingdom, as though they were lyrical gems of the first order. " Can such things be?" Is the throne of Taste to be thus usurped by a host of illiterate scribblers? Are such productions, abounding with Cockney slang, *double entendres,* and indelicate allusions, to be longer tolerated? Forbid it, shade of the immortal Burns,! It is high time such nonsensical rubbish as " *Vilikens and his Dinah,*" " *Billy Barlow,*" and the " *Ratcatcher's Daughter,*" was discountenanced, and a higher and more refined taste evinced for genuine songs of an elevating nature, pure in sentiment, rich in natural feeling, and bearing the impress of having sprung spontaneous from the depths of the poet's heart.

The following vulgar effusion is a specimen of the songs just alluded to :—

Illustration.

BILLY TAYLOR.

Billy Taylor was a gay young feller
  Full of fun and full of glee,
And his heart he did diskiver
  To a lady fair and free,
          Tiddy, iddy, &c.

(Spoken.) This werse describes how he fell a wictim to the liberty of the press.

Four and twenty stout young fellers,
   Clad they were in blue array,
Came and pressed poor Billy Taylor,
   And off to sea bore him away.
            Tiddy, iddy, &c.

(Spoken.) The next werse tells wot his true love resolved
to do, and how she did it.
   Soon his true love followed arter,
      Under the name of Richard Carr,
   And her lily-vite hands she daubed all over
      Vith the nasty pitch and tar.
            Tiddy, iddy, &c.

(Spoken.) The next werse describes wot wasn't wisible
when she went aboard the wessel.
   But she was wounded in the first engagement
      When fighting like a man among the rest,
   And they diskiver'd her sex-uation
      When she came to be undressed.
            Tiddy, iddy, &c.

(Spoken.) This werse tells you how the capting had his
weather-eye open.
   The capting was every inch a sailor,
      Says he, " What wind has blown you here ?"
   Says she, " I'm looking for Billy Taylor,
      Whom you pressed and I love dear."
            Tiddy, iddy, &c.

Other verses succeed too contemptible and indelicate to quote.

For some years past another class of compositions

misnamed " *Negro Melodies*," have inundated the
musical world. These effusions, though occasionally
wed to good music, are, generally speaking, miserable
abortions as regards possessing any poetic merit.
They emanate from the Metropolis, and are written
by Cockneys who never beheld the " Ohio," and who
know nothing whatever of the scenes and manners
they pretend to delineate ; and yet, strange to say,
these melodies have been sung at our principal places
of amusement through the length and breadth of the
land. Even since the days when "*Jump Jim Crow*,"
became popular, and it was nightly sung in London by
Mr. Rice, parties styling themselves " *Ethiopean
Serenaders*," *African Troupes*," &c. have taken the
tour of the provinces, and though picked from the
metropolitan singing saloons they have professed to
give true representations of negro life and character!
Togged out in seedy black suits, with white cravats,
curly wigs, and blackened faces, they have attempted
by unnatural grimaces, and winks, and nods, and
stale conundrums, to impose on the gullibility of
poor simple John Bull. These wandering minstrels,
however, with their doleful banjos, have had their
day—the negro ditties, with their broken English,
are fast sinking in public estimation, and in a short
time, it is hoped, they will descend into utter oblivion,
and be replaced by others of a more refined and elevating nature.

We turn now to the lyrics of Tennyson, and
other distinguished poets of the present day. The
fame of Tennyson has been gradually increasing

during the last thirty years. His genius is retros-
pective; and though not so popular as our greater
poets who have passed the bourne of life, yet he is
undoubtedly the best "poet of the age." He has won
the poet's crown, and he has won it honorably. His
first volume of poems he published so far back as
1830. About four years afterwards he produced another volume. Both these volumes being severely
criticised in some of the leading reviews, his Muse
remained silent for eight years. He then reprinted
them, much altered and improved, with several addi-
tional pieces. Subsequently he has published many
poems of superior merit, all of which have had a
favorable reception.

The style of Tennyson is particularly quaint, yet
always graceful and elegant. His greatest characteristic is a beautiful simplicity. He has neither the
fervency of Campbell nor the passion of Byron. His
poetry is calm and meditative. It flows like a placid
brook gliding gently along through " quiet meadows"
and " sighing reeds," where nothing interrupts the
even tenor of its way. He embodies in his verse
the deepest thoughts in the most simple language,
and many of his poems, such as " *Mariana in the
moated grange,*" breathe the very soul of sadness, as
though, at times, he felt in his heart the "charm
of melancholy."

The following ballads, selected from his early
poems, exhibit much poetic power combined with
extreme simplicity of diction ;—

Illustration.

THE MILLER'S DAUGHTER.

It is the miller's daughter,
  And she is grown so dear, so dear,
That I would be the jewel
  That trembles at her ear:
For hid in ringlets day and night,
I'd touch her neck so warm and white.

And I would be the girdle
  About her dainty dainty waist,
And her heart would beat against me,
  In sorrow and in rest:
And I should know if it beat right,
I'd clasp it round so close and tight.

And I would be the necklace,
  And all day long to fall and rise
Upon her balmy bosom
  With her laughter or her sighs,
And I would lie so light, so light,
I scarce should be unclasp'd at night.

———

Illustration.

NEW YEAR'S EVE.

If you're waking call me early, call me early, mother dear.
For I would see the sun rise upon the glad New-year.
It is the last New-year that I shall ever see,
Then you may lay me low i' the mould and think no more of me.

To-night I saw the sun set: he set and left behind
The good old year, the dear old time, and all my peace of mind;
And the New-year's coming up, mother, but I shall never see
The blossom on the blackthorn, the leaf upon the tree.

Last May we made a crown of flowers : we had a merry day :
Beneath the hawthorn on the green they made me Queen of May ;
And we danced about the may-pole and in the hazel copse,
Till Charles's Wain came out above the tall white chimney-tops.

There's not a flower on all the hills: the frost is on the pane :
I only wish to live till the snowdrops come again ;
I wish the snow would melt and the sun come out on high :
I long to see a flower so before the day I die.

The building rook 'ill caw from the windy tall elm-tree,
And the tufted plover pipe along the fallow lea,
And the swallow 'ill come back again with summer o'er the wave,
But I shall lie alone, mother, within the mouldering grave.

Upon the chancel-casement, and upon that grave of mine,
In the early early morning the summer sun 'ill shine,
Before the red cock crows from the farm upon the hill,
When you are warm-asleep, mother, and all the world is still.

When the flowers come again, mother, beneath the waning light
You'll never see me more in the long gray fields at night ;
When from the dry dark wold the summer airs blow cool
On the oat-grass, and the sword-grass, and the bulrush in the pool.

You'll bury me, my mother, just beneath the hawthorn shade,
And you'll come sometimes and see me where I am lowly laid.
I shall not forget you, mother, I shall hear you when you pass,
With your feet above my head in the long and pleasant grass.

I have been wild and wayward, but you'll forgive me now ;
You'll kiss me, my own mother. and forgive me ere I go :
Nay, nay, you must not weep, nor let your grief be wild,
You should not fret for me, mother, you have another child.

If I can I'll come again, mother, from out my resting-place ;
Tho' you'll not see me, mother, I shall look upon your face ;
Tho' I cannot speak a word, I shall harken what you say,
And be often, often with you when you think I'm far away.

Goodnight, goodnight, when I have said goodnight for evermore,
And you see me carried out from the threshold of the door;
Don't let Effie come to see me till my grave be growing green :
She'll be a better child to you than ever I have been.

She'll find my garden-tools upon the granary floor :
Let her take 'em : they are hers : I shall never garden more :
But tell her, when I'm gone, to train the rose-bush that I set
About the parlour-window and the box of mignonette.

Good-night, sweet mother : call me before the day is born,
All night I lie awake, but I fall asleep at morn ;
But I would see the sun rise upon the glad New-year,
So, if you're waking, call me, call me early, mother dear.

————

Many of our living poets, though considered
inferior in genius to Tennyson, have greatly enriched our literature with lyrics which shew them to
be graceful and elegant writers, and men of refined
feeling as well as undoubted taste.   Amongst this
number may be included Bryan Walter Procter, who
has produced many beautiful effusions under the
assumed name of Barry Cornwall—Thomas K. Hervey,
a sweet poet—Charles Swain, author of " The Mind,"
W. Monckton Milnes, M. P.—D. M. Moir, better
known as the Delta of Blackwood's Magazine—and
Gerald Massey.

The next extract is very touching and beautiful. It is from the pen of D. M. Moir, on the death of
his infant son, three years old, on whom the pet
name of " Casa Wappy" had been self-conferred.

Illustration.

CASA WAPPY.

And hast thou sought thy heavenly home,
  Our fond dear boy—
The realms where sorrow dare not come,
  Where life is joy?
Pure at thy death as at thy birth,
Thy spirit caught no taint from earth;
Even by its bliss we mete our death,
          Casa Wappy!

Despair was in our last farewell,
  As closed thine eye;
Tears of our anguish may not tell
  When thou didst die;
Words may not paint our grief for thee,
Sighs are but bubbles on the sea
Of our unfathomed agony,
          Casa Wappy!

Thou wert a vision of delight
  To bless us given;
Beauty embodied to our sight,
  A type of heaven:
So dear to us thou wert, thou art
Even less thine own self than a part
Of mine and of thy mother's heart,
          Casa Wappy!

Thy bright brief day knew no decline,
  'Twas cloudless joy;
Sunrise and night alone were thine,
  Beloved boy!
This morn beheld thee blithe and gay,
That found thee prostrate in decay,
And ere a third shone, clay was clay,
          Casa Wappy!

         *   *   *

We mourn for thee when blind blank night
   The chamber fills ;
We pine for thee when morn's first light
   Reddens the hills :
The sun, the moon, the stars, the sea,
All, to the wall-flower and wild pea,
Are changed—we saw the world through thee,
        Casa Wappy !

And though, perchance, a smile may gleam
   Of casual mirth,
It doth not own whate'er may seem,
   An inward birth :
We miss thy small step on the stair ;
We miss thee at thine evening prayer !
All day we miss thee, everywhere,
        Casa Wappy !

Snows muffled earth when thou didst go,
   In life's spring bloom,
Down to the appointed house below,
   The silent tomb,
But now the green leaves of the tree,
The cuckoo and ' the busy bee,'
Return—but with them bring not thee,
        Casa Wappy !

'Tis so ; but can it be (while flowers
   Revive again)—
Man's doom, in death that we and ours
   For aye remain ?
Oh ! can it be, that o'er the grave
The grass renewed, should yearly wave,
Yet God forget our child to save ?—
        Casa Wappy !

It cannot be : for were it so
   Thus man could die,
Life were a mockery, Thought were wo,
   And Truth a lie ;
Heaven were a coinage of the brain,
Religion frenzy, Virtue vain,
And all our hopes to meet again,
        Casa Wappy !

Then be to us, O dear, lost child !
  With beam of love,
A star, death's uncongenial wild
  Smiling above ;
Soon, soon thy little feet have trod
The skyward path, the seraph's road,
That led the back from man to God,
          Casa Wappy!

Yet 'tis sweet balm to our despair,
  Fond, fairest boy,
That heaven is God's, and thou art there,
  With him in joy :
There past are death and all its woes,
There beauty's stream for ever flows,
And pleasure's day no sunset knows.
          Casa Wappy !

Farewell, then—for a while, farewell—
  Pride of my heart !
It cannot be that long we dwell,
  Thus torn apart :
Time's shadows like the shuttle flee :
And, dark howe'er life's night may be,
Beyond the grave I'll meet with thee,
          Casa Wappy !

The youngest of the living poets previously alluded to is Gerald Massey. He is a lyrist of the
greatest promise. In many features of his genius,
Walter Savage observes, "he bears a marvellous
resemblance to Keats." He has been designated " the
poet of the people." He sings " heart-stirring and
melodious songs—songs of Liberty and Love, coming
warmly from the heart," and the latter so pure and
sweet as oft to rival the best love strains of Burns.
As a lyrist of superior power Gerald Massey at present stands high. Already he has reaped a rich har-

vest and fame, and in all probability he is destined to earn for himself a crown of immortality. In the preface to the third edition of " *Babe Christabel*," he states, when speaking on this subject, " that the dearth of Poetry should be great in a country where we hail as poets such as have been crowned of late. For myself," he continues, " I have only entered the lists and inscribed my name; the race has yet to be run. Whether I shall run it, and win the Poet's crown, or not, time alone will prove, and not the prediction of friend or foe. The crowns of Poetry are not in the keeping of critics. There have been many who have given some signs of promise—just set a rainbow of hope in the dark cloud of their life—and have never fulfilled their promise ; and the world has wondered why. I hope that my future holds some happier fate. I think there is a work for me to do, and I trust to accomplish it."

Thus speaks the author of " *Babe Christabel*" ; but with due deference to his remarks, we beg to observe, that though he still is young, though his early years were passed in the deepest poverty, deprived of all scholastic instruction except what a penny school afforded, and though, when more advanced in years, he had to labour with his own hands for a very bare subsistence ; yet, by his perseverance and genius, he has surmounted the obstacles that retarded his onward progress, and at length, climbing the steep of Parnassus with the easy grace and bearing of a conqueror, he has far out-distanced his youthful and less gifted compeers in the race for lyrical fame.

The poetry of Gerald Massey is highly exuberant in imagery, and healthful in freshness like a sweet morning in Spring. He is the champion of Freedom, and his war odes in her cause are splendid compositions. He sings them with a brave English heart and an unshackled mind, like one not to be cowed down by the carping of critics or any one else. They contain strong words and burning thoughts that flash in almost every line like volleys from the "red artillery" as the "combat deepens." But how great the contrast when he sings of love and beauty. How gentle, how extremely tender, and how full of feeling his effusions then are! Devoid of any meretricious ornament, they glow profusely with the sweetest flowers of Poesy.

The following production is selected from his love lyrics:—

—

Illustration.

NO JEWELLED BEAUTY IS MY LOVE.

No jewelled beauty is my love,
    Yet in her earnest face,
There's such a world of tenderness
    She needs no other grace.
Her smiles and voice around my life
    In light and music twine,
And dear, O very dear to me
    Is this sweet love of mine.

O joy! to know there's one fond heart
    Beats ever true to me;
It sets mine leaping like a lyre,
    In sweetest melody;

My soul upsprings a Deity
  To hear her voice divine ;
And dear, O very dear to me,
  Is this sweet Love of mine.

If ever I have sighed for wealth,
  'Twas all for her I trow ;
And if I win Fame's victor wreath
  I'll twine it round her brow.
There may be forms more beautiful,
  And souls of Summer shine,
But none, O none, so dear to me,
  As this sweet Love of mine.

The preceding verses are a fair specimen of the
love strains of Gerald Massey. Our next selection is
a lyric which shows him in a more pathetic mood. It
is entitled "Little Willie," and a sweet production it
is. "Little Willie" was a poor boy, nearly related to
Massey, and he died in the parish workhouse when
the poet was sunk in the deepest poverty. The pity-
ing heart of Massey, no doubt, felt deeply when he
learnt that the little sufferer, whom he loved, had

> "From the cold world
>   Crouched down to die,"

Where his remains, alas, found their final resting-
place—a workhouse grave.

Illustration.

LITTLE WILLIE.

Poor little Willie,
  With his many pretty wiles ;
Worlds of wisdom in his looks,
  And quaint, quiet smiles ;

Hair of amber, touched with
    Gold of heaven so brave ;
All lying darkly hid
    In a workhouse grave.

You remember little Willie ;
    Fair and funny fellow he !
Sprang like a lily
    From the dirt of Poverty.
Poor little Willie !
    Not a friend was nigh,
When, from the cold world,
    He crouched down to die.

In the day we wandered foodless,
    Little Willie cried for bread ;
In the night we wandered homeless,
    Little Willie cried for bed,
Parted at the Workhouse door,
    Not a word we said ;
Ah ! so tired was little Willie,
    And so sweetly sleep the dead.

'Twas in the dead of Winter
    We laid him in the earth ;
The world brought in the new year
    On a tide of mirth :
But, for lost little Willie,
    Not a tear we crave ;
Cold and hunger cannot wake him
    In a Workhouse grave.

We thought him beautiful,
    Felt it hard to part ;
We loved him dutiful ;
    Down, down, poor heart !
The storms they may beat,
    The winter winds may rave,
Little Willie feels them not
    In a Workhouse grave.

No room for little Willie;
   In the world he had no part;
On him stared the Gorgon eye
   Through which looks no heart.
Come to me, said Heaven;
   And, if Heaven will save,
It little matters though the door
   Be a Workhouse grave.

Such effusions as the foregoing, so full of natural feeling and graceful excellence, are worthy the nation that has given birth to a Shakspere and a Burns. The poetic element, it seems, is not yet extinct amongst us. Our present popular lyrists, with Tennyson at their head, are yet held in the highest estimation, though lights of greater magnitude have not appeared since the days of Wordsworth. We hail, therefore, with the greatest gratification, their endeavours to charm and instruct us—we hail with pleasure every attempt made to encourage a correct taste for good music united to "immortal verse."

In our pilgrimage through life Music and Poetry have been to us a consolation and a joy. They have cheered us in the hour of sorrow—they have consoled us in the day of misfortune. They are also connected in our mind, with many pleasing reminiscences and associations, and we may justly add, with some of the happiest moments we ever enjoyed. They are to the intellectual world what the glad sunshine, the gay flowers, and all that is beautiful in Creation are in the natural world. Music is of heavenly origin, and her divine sister, Poetry, is the acknowledged civilizer of the human race. Hand in hand they con-

tribute to brighten our existence as the dispensers of
pure and rational enjoyment. May we more and more,
then, be induced to cultivate a taste for them. May
their influence be felt in every bosom—in the social
circle as well as at our own firesides, where they are
best appreciated ;—so that they may ever continue
to charm and delight us, to refine our feelings, to elevate our thoughts, and expand our affections to admire
whatever is truly great and good in human nature,
and whatever is lovely and delightful to behold when
we contemplate the wondrous works of Him who
laid the foundations of the earth, and bid

> " The spangled heavens, a shining frame,
>   Their great Original proclaim,
>   For ever singing as they shine,
>   The hand that made us is divine !"

The Genius and Lyrics of Burns.

CHAPTER VII.

Introductory Remarks.

There is a class of writers who have advanced innumerable arguments to prove, that in the human species there is originally no intellectual superiority of one over another—that in all men there is no innate capacity, and, consequently, there is no such thing as genius in the world. These writers affirm, that the great superiority of intellect one person has above another is entirely owing to circumstances which tend, by assiduity and perseverance, to mature the mind and expand the understanding. Another class of writers, amongst whom are some of the most profound metaphysicians this country ever produced, have as stubbornly contended that genius is innate, and, in consequence, that some men have naturally a genius for one thing and some for another. The latter is the generally received opinion, and with this opinion we cordially agree, as we can come to no

other conclusion than that it is correct.   What was it,
we ask, but the mighty power of genius, united to
close observation, that enabled Shakspere to form his
wonderful creations—that urged Newton to investi-
gate the dark and hidden mysteries of nature—that
inspired Herscell to scale, through the illimitable
bounds of space, the starry heavens—that prompted
Watt to develop the astonishing powers of steam—
and that instigated a host of other distinguished
characters to soar far beyond the ordinary capacity of
men and bequeath us the richest legacies of undying
thought and the most masterly productions of scien-
tific skill ?

Amongst this pre-eminently gifted number stands
ROBERT BURNS, the Shakspere of Scotland, who, in the
latter part of the last century, like the refulgent sun
emerging from a cloud, burst from his obscurity, and
not only astonished his own admiring countrymen,
but the whole of the literati of the age, with his
matchless productions, which, for natural beauty and
exquisite sweetness, have not been surpassed since he
himself, in the language of Wordsworth, "walked
in glory and in joy behind the plough." Yes, com-
muning with his own glorious thoughts, he walked
behind the plough, and there catching the light of
inspiration from Nature herself, he truthfully depicted,
in undying strains, the joys and the sorrows, the loves
and the toils of the peasantry of his own country. His
mission as a poet was to elevate their condition, and
no man was better qualified for the task. "By sparks
from his etherial soul he wished to elevate their

spiritual natures, and make them in love with all that is pure, and good, and beautiful on the earth." In his character there was no selfishness, no hypocritical bowing down to the titled great, no " Pride that soars, and meanness that licks the dust." Whatever were his failings no charge of this kind was ever made against his character. Inheriting from his birth a proud spirit, and conscious of his own intellectual power, he walked the earth one of Nature's nobility, acknowledging, as it were, no superior. Though nursed in the lap of Poverty, though in his after years he had to struggle with adversity and disappointed hopes of every shape; yet to the last hour of his eventful life the independence of his spirit was never crushed, his integrity never sullied, his manly worth never demeaned. These noble attributes were enthroned in his heart, where, under all circumstances, they ever retained a seat, even when in the full blaze of his fame he shone an intellectual meteor at the gay coteries of " titled dukes and jewelled duchesses," where the honour paid to his genius, says Dugald Stewart, " would have turned any head but his own."

But after being lionised, if we may use the expression, in almost every circle of rank and fashion in the metropolis of Scotland, after having enjoyed the society of her greatest men in the republic of letters, who were more astonished, it is said, at the power of his eloquence than even the beauty of his poems, the novelty of his appearance amongst them gradually wore away; and poor, neglected Burns, the greatest poet Scotland ever produced, with his pro-

pects blasted, his name traduced, and his proud
heart stung to the quick by unmerited coldness, was
obliged, in a spirit of dejection, to return to that
plough where the poetic genius of his country found
him.   Yes, poor, unfortunate Burns, the man whose
poems had so charmed his countrymen—the man
whom the higher classes had so feasted, whose com-
pany they had so courted, and whose eloquence had
so astonished them, was obliged to return to the
plough to earn for himself an honest Independence
by the labour of his own hands, having learnt this
important lesson, that men in every station of society,
whether in high life or low, are much about the same.

> " Mourn, guilty Scotland, mourn !
> Bow to the dust in widowed shame,
> Hide thee in sackcloth, with dishevelled hair ;
> But wreath around the urn of Burns
> No mournful yew—the laughing thorn, his claim,
> Twined with harebell and daisy, let him wear."

CHAPTER VIII.

Burns as the poet of the Beautiful.

As a poet Burns is universally acknowledged to
rank amongst the best masters of the lyre ; and well
worthy is he of this high distinction, for in the whole
range of British literature where can we find enshrined
more endearing memorials of poetic talent than he has
left us.   In his poems we meet with no unnatural
conceits, no sickening sentimentality ; but, strewed

with a prolific hand, we find his productions abounding with sentiments that "give the world assurance of A MAN"—sentiments that exalt our souls, that make our hearts glow within us, so that while we feel their freshness, their vigour, and their beauty and truthfulness, we are at a loss which to admire most—the genius of the heaven-taught bard who gave birth to such glorious conceptions, or the brave and manly heart that gave them utterance.

The genius of Burns was entirely original. It needed no borrowed lustre to improve it. Unlike that of many of our bards it stooped to the subject it embellished, and so illimitable was its range that in a moment he could change from "grave to gay, from lively to severe," from the ludicrous to the terrible, from the simple to the sublime. The versatility of his powers is best shown in "Tam O'Shanter," which displays all these qualities in rapid succession. Sir Walter Scott, says of Burns, that "no poet, with the exception of Shakspere, ever possessed the power of exciting the most varied and discordant emotions in such rapid succession." Confined to no species of composition, his genius alike shone on whatever subject he touched, no matter how various its features. It combined the humour of Pindar, the sublimity of Milton, the vigour of Junius, and the moral power and withering satire of Pope. As a didactic poet and satirist Burns excels all other bards. He has made the Ayr, the Nith, and the "bonnie Doon" classic streams. The fair maidens who attracted his attention on their "banks and braes" he has immor-

talised in song. These maidens were his Muses—
their beauty gave him inspiration. As he described
their loveliness, their purity, their delicacy of sentiment, and other charms, he invested them with every
feminine excellence according to his own ideal notions
of what a lovely woman ought to be.

Burns associated with woman whatever was delightful to behold in the material world. To heighten
her beauty by analogy he sought for images amongst
the loveliest objects on the varied face of Nature.
It is this association which forms the great secret of
his power to charm the popular heart, and this it is
which distinguishes him, in the highest degree, as the
poet of the beautiful.

The greatest element in the genius of Burns was
his admiration of the beautiful, the strongest trait in
his nature was to love—to love all things with a
loving heart, no matter how lowly. He delighted,
therefore, to draw moral truths from the most trivial
things that crossed his path—he loved to describe
cottage life in all its holy beauty and purity, and to
sing of woman, "lovely woman," as though she were
a divinity without one human imperfection. A love
for the beautiful, the pure, and the good, in all their
various phases, was centred in his heart, and thus, it
may be said, he was constituted to adorn all he touched.

The truth of these remarks is best illustrated by
his tender "Address to a Mountain Daisy." This
simple flower, which

"Died to prove
The tender charm of poetry and love,"

He met in the furrowed field, when, with glorious thoughts, far beyond his occupation, he "walked behind the plough," as it bloomed in beauty on the mountain side. Its "crimson-tipped" crest met his attentive eye, and crushing its slender stem "amang the stoure," he then, in the moment of inspiration, his heart melting with the soft sympathies of his nature, elegised its fate in immortal strains.

—

Illustration.

TO A MOUNTAIN DAISY.

Wee, modest, crimson-tipped flow'r,
Thou's met me in an evil hour,
For I maun crush amang the stoure
      Thy slender stem :
To spare thee now is past my pow'r,
      Thou bonnie gem.

Alas ! it's no thy neebor sweet,
The bonnie lark, companion meet !
Bending thee 'mang the dewy weet !
      Wi' spreckl'd breast,
When upward-springing, blythe, to greet,
      The purpling east.

Cauld blew the bitter-biting north
Upon thy early, humble birth ;
Yet cheerfully thou glinted forth
      Amid the storm,
Scarce rear'd above the parent earth
      Thy tender form.

The flaunting flowers our gardens yield,
High shelt'ring woods and wa's maun shield ;
But thou, beneath the random bield
      O' clod or stane,
Adorns the histie stibble-field
      Unseen, alane.

There, in thy scanty mantle clad,
Thy snawie bosom sunward spread,
Thou lifts thy unassuming head
        In humble guise ;
But now the share uptears thy bed,
        And low thou lies !

Such is the fate of artless maid,
Sweet flow'ret of the rural shade !
By love's simplicity betray'd,
        And guileless trust,
'Till she, like thee, all soil'd, is laid
        Low i' the dust.

Such is the fate of simple bard,
On life's rough ocean luckless starr'd !
Unskilful he to note the card
        Of prudent lore,
'Till billows rage, and gales blow hard,
        And whelm him o'er !

Such fate to suffering worth is giv'n,
Who long with wants and woes has striv'n,
By human pride or cunning driv'n
        To mis'ry's brink.
Till wrench'd of every stay but Heav'n,
        He, ruin'd, sink !

Ev'n thou who mourn'st the Daisy's fate,
That fate is thine—no distant date ;
Stern Ruin's ploughshare drives, elate,
        Full on thy bloom,
Till crush'd beneath the furrow's weight,
        Shall be thy doom !

What beautiful moral deductions are associated with the fate of this " wee, modest, crimson-tipped flower !" How tender in sentiment, how felicitous in expression is every verse ! But take these deductions from the verses and they would lose the charm with which genius has invested them.

Burns composed the preceding poem when as a husbandman he received wages amounting only to seven pounds a year. Such a production from one whose livelihood was obtained by the sweat of his brow, whose home was the "cauld clay biggin" that gave him birth, and whose companions were merely the simple rustics of his native vale, may well excite our astonishment—but what is there that genius cannot accomplish? Burns, however, in addition to his gifted genius, possessed in his manly breast a heart whence flowed, in his moods of mournfulness, the most exquisite tenderness. For deep pathos and purity of thought where can we find poems to surpass his Ode to "*Mary in Heaven*" or his sweet song of "*Highland Mary?*" These beautiful compositions will for ever stand as monuments to the memory of the being whose premature death Burns so tenderly bewailed, and whose image he retained within his "bosom's core" to the latest day of his existence,

> " For dear to him as light and life
> Was his sweet Highland Mary."

In Burns's earliest journal, after complimenting the genius of the bards who composed our ancient ballads, and whose very names are buried among the wreck of things that were, we find this beautiful passage, which powerfully shows how deeply he lamented the death of his Highland Mary. " O ye illustrious names unknown, who could feel so strongly, and

describe so well; the last, the meanest of the Muse's
train—one who, though far inferior to your flights,
yet eyes your path, and, with trembling wing, would
sometimes soar after you—a poor, rustic bard, unknown, pays this sympathetic pang to your memory.
Some of you tell us, with all the charms of verse,
that you have been unfortunate in the world—unfortunate in love—he too has felt the loss of his fortune,
the loss of friends; but, *worst of all, the loss of the
woman he adored.*"   When Burns wrote these words
he deeply felt, no doubt, in his own mind the loss of
his Highland Mary, the being above all others whom
he most loved.   The song of "*Highland Mary*" and
his lines "*To Mary in Heaven*" are sufficient of themselves to stamp him as the poet of the Beautiful.

Illustration.

TO MARY IN HEAVEN.

Thou ling'ring star, with less'ning ray,
    That lov'st to greet the early morn,
Again thou usherest in the day
    My Mary from my soul was torn.
O Mary! dear departed shade!
    Where is thy place of blissful rest?
See'st thou thy lover lowly laid?
    Hear'st thou the groans that rend his breast?

That sacred hour can I forget,
    Can I forget the hallowed grove,
Where by the winding Ayr we met,
    To live one day of parting love!

Eternity cannot efface
   Those records dear of transports past ;
Thy image at our last embrace ;
   Ah! little thought we 'twas our last!

Ayr, gurgling, kiss'd his pebbled shore,
   O'erhung with wild woods, thick'ning green ;
The fragrant birch, and hawthorn hoar,
   Twin'd am'rous round the raptur'd scene ;
The flow'rs sprang wanton to be prest,
   The birds sang love on every spray—
Till too, too soon, the glowing west
   Proclaim'd the speed of winged day.

Still o'er these scenes my mem'ry wakes,
   And fondly broods with miser care !
Time but th' impression stronger makes,
   As streams their channels deeper wear.
My Mary, dear departed shade !
   Where is thy place of blissful rest ?
See'st thou thy lover lowly laid ?
   Hear'st thou the groans that rend his breast ?

———

These mournful stanzas were composed by Burns
one evening at twilight when his heart was sad, and
his thoughts reverted to his Highland Mary, as he
lay on some loose sheaves in the stack yard, gazing
on a bright, particular star in the sky. He never forgot his early attachment to her ; for, we find, that
many years after her death, when he had long been
married and had a family to support, he thus spoke
of her, in a letter to Mrs. Dunlop :—" If there is another life, it must be only for the just, the benevolent,
the amiable, and the humane. What a flattering idea,
then, is a world to come ! There shall I, with speech-
less rapture, again recognise my lost, my ever dear

Mary, whose bosom was fraught with truth, honour, constancy, and love."

The next illustration we have selected, to show that Burns is the poet of the Beautiful, is the song "*Of a' the airts the wind can blaw*," which ranks amongst his best productions. Though he has said, "that Hymen was not the divinity he invoked when he wrote any of his love songs;" yet, it was after he had married his "lovely Jean" that he composed this song in her praise, and a sweeter offering genius could not have presented to her whom he had vowed at the altar to love and to cherish. He composed it when on a visit to Mossgiel, even before the honeymoon had waned, and when her image, no doubt, was constantly in his mind. On his return home he presented this composition to his "Jean," and in the evening he had the pleasure of hearing her sing it. Thus the amiable being that inspired the lay was the first that warbled it with her "wood notes wild."

Mrs. Burns died in the year 1834, in the 70th year of her age, having survived her husband 38 years. She always spoke of him with the greatest respect, and as one of the kindest of husbands. At his demise she was placed by the generosity of the British nation in comfortable circumstances at Dumfries, where she lived respected, and died lamented for the gentleness of her nature and the amiability of her disposition.

Illustration.

OF A' THE AIRTS THE WIND CAN BLAW.

—

Of a' the airts the wind can blaw
    I dearly like the west,
For there the bonnie lassie lives,
    The lassie I lo'e best :
There wild woods grow and rivers row,
    And mony a hill between ;
By day and night my fancy's flight
    Is ever wi' my Jean.

I see her in the dewy flowers,
    I see her sweet and fair ;
I hear her in the tunefu' birds,
    I hear her charm the air :
There's not a bonnie flower that springs
    By fountain, shaw, or green,
There's not a bonnie bird that sings
    But minds me o' my Jean.

O blaw, ye westlin winds, blaw soft,
    Amang the leafy trees,
Wi' balmy gale, frae hill and dale,
    Bring hame the laden bees ;
And bring the lassie back to me
    That's aye sae neat and clean ;
Ae smile o' her wad banish care,
    Sae charming is my Jean.

What sighs and vows amang the knowes
    Hae passed atween us twa !
How fond to meet, how wae to part,
    That night she gaed awa !
The powers aboon can only ken,
    To whom the heart is seen,
That nane can be so dear to me
    As my sweet lovely Jean !

It is generally allowed by those who have commented on the poetic genius of Burns that his numerous songs on the subject of Love are the sweetest of his productions, and that they embody more of the beautiful than can be found in his other effusions. This may be imputed to the fact, that the greater number of them were written during the latter part of his life when his judgment had become matured. These productions, therefore, are consequently distinguished by that superior polish and elegance of expression, which, in general, we do not find in the earlier efforts of his Muse.

Some of the most poetical of these lyrics he wrote in praise of Miss Jessy Lewars, a young lady of much modesty and loveliness, who, like a " ministering angel," attended him with all the care and affection of a daughter, during his long, last, fatal illness. These poetic gems may be considered, therefore, as the poet's songs of gratitude to this lady for the kind offices she performed for him and his family in the hour of sickness. They were written when the suffering bard was gradually sinking, and they thus powerfully shew that as he departed from amongst us his genius shone to the very last, like day's bright luminary setting in a blaze of glory.

How beautiful are the following verses which the dying poet wrote in honour of this lady, whom he has immortalized :

Illustration.

J E S S Y.

—

Here's a health to ane I lo'e dear ;
　　Here's a health to ane I lo'e dear ;
Thou art sweet as the smile when fond lovers meet,
　　And soft as their parting tear—Jessy !

Altho' thou maun never be mine,
　　Altho' even hope is denied :
'Tis sweeter for thee despairing,
　　Than aught in the world beside—Jessy !

I mourn through the gay, gaudy day,
　　As, hopeless, I muse on thy charms ;
But welcome the dream o' sweet slumber,
　　For then I am lockt in thy arms—Jessy !

I guess by the dear angel smile,
　　I guess by the love-rolling e'e ;
But why urge the tender confession
　　'Gainst fortune's fell cruel decree ?—Jessy !

Here's a health to ane I lo'e dear ;
　　Here's a health to ane I lo'e dear ;
Thou art sweet as the smile when fond lovers meet,
　　And soft as their parting tear—Jessy !

———

One day Burns strongly solicited Jessy Lewars
to play on the piano-forte one of her favorite old
Scotch airs, and he promised to compose words to it
complimentary to her. The poet was then very far
reduced by sickness, and the young lady to oblige
him sat down to the instrument. After playing an

old Scotch air three or four times over, he hummed it awhile, and then in a few minutes he composed the song of " *O wert thou in the cauld blast*," which forms the next illustration to show that Burns is the the poet of the beautiful.

Many years after this little incident took place, when Burns shone a bright star in the galaxy of Fame and the once lovely Jessy Lewars had become an aged widow, this song attracted the attention of Felix Mendelssohn, the great German composer, who was passionately fond of the music of Scotland. He was particularly struck with the beautiful sentiments so well expressed in this song—he saw that it expressed even more than common love—that it displayed the outpourings of a grateful heart—and, in consequence, he married the words to music which he composed, and which breathes the very soul of tragic mournfulness. We are indebted, therefore, for this sweet composition to the genius of Burns, the goodness of Jessy Lewars, and the musical talent of Mendelsshon.

Illustration.

OH, WERT THOU IN THE CAULD BLAST.

Oh, wert thou in the cauld blast,
   On yonder lea, on yonder lea,
My plaidie to the angry airt,
   I'd shelter thee, I'd shelter thee ;
Or did Misfortune's bitter storms
   Around thee blaw, around thee blaw,
Thy beild should be my bosom,
   To share it a', to share to a'.

Or were I in the wildest waste,
  Sae black and bare, sae black and bare,
The desert were a paradise
  If thou wert there, if thou were there :
Or were I monarch o' the globe,
  Wi' thee to reign, wi' thee to reign,
The brightest jewel in my crown
  Wad be my queen, wad be my queen.

CHAPTER IX.

Burns as the Poet of the Humorous and the Social.

Having briefly noticed the great power that Burns possessed in depicting the beautiful in creation, we shall now proceed to speak of him as the poet of the Humorous and the Social ; for with the comprehensive and varied powers of his genius he could with the greatest facility, as previously observed, pass from "grave to gay," from the deepest pathos to the broadest humour, so as to electrify every social circle with the originality and vividness of his conceptions, and the glowing energy of his eloquence. Whatever the circle he honoured with his presence he was the delight of all, the distinguished "guest of guests," the "bright, particular star" to which every eye was directed, to which every heart paid the homage of admiration. To enjoy the rich strokes of his humour, to catch the electric flashes of his wit, to hear a man

" endowed with the most divine power of speech of any Briton of the age," it is stated, that reapers would quit their work, the cobbler would leave his last, the smith his smithy, ostlers and waiters would hurry out of bed, squires would travel for miles, and titled lords and "jewelled duchesses" would invite him to their feasts.

There was not a man in all Scotland that possessed such conversational powers, or had a kinder heart or a more social disposition than Burns—there was not a man in all Scotland who would not have felt honoured by having him under his roof. But however he might be flattered by the attentions of the titled and the great, it was the peasantry of his own country that most esteemed him for his worth and most honoured him for his genius. He had been born and bred amongst them—he had associated with them—he had felt as they had felt. He had described their joys, their sorrows, and their virtues, and showed that there could be pure holy love and Christian piety beneath the thatched roof of the most humble cotter. As a man they loved him for the generosity of his nature and the independence of his spirit, and as a poet they admired him for the hold which the beauty and truthfulness of his compositions had on their hearts.

Professor Wilson, when speaking on this subject, eloquently observes, "But who were they in his own country who continued stedfastly to honour his genius and himself? The men of his own order, the WORKING PEOPLE. Whatever the instruments of their toil, they

patronised him then—they patronise him now—they
would not hurt a hair of his head—they will not hear of
any dishonour to his dust—they know full well what
it is to endure, to yield, to enjoy, and to suffer, and
the memory of their own bard will be honoured for
ever among the brotherhood like a religion."

But to return to the humour and sociability of
Burns. No man was ever by nature more highly
gifted with these qualities. His sociality was warm
and unrestrained, his humour so rich and racy that
on all occasions he was "wont to set the table in a
roar."

When Burns was at Edinbro' he was often invited to the splendid suppers then given, after the
manner of the ancients, by that eccentric noble-
man, Lord Monboddo. At one of these entertain-
ments a select party was assembled, by hislordship's
special invitation, purposely to see and to hear the
wonderful ploughman of Kyle. During the repast,
which was magnificent beyond description, his Lordship presided

"In all the starch formalities of state."

His demeanour on the occasion was so distant, so
formal, and so aristocratic, that his guests were all
nearly awed into complete silence. On the removal
of the cloth, the juice of the grape began to circulate
in decanters of a Grecian shape, wreathed in flowers ;
but not so the genial current in the veins of the warm-
hearted Burns. His lordship's deportment was so
extremely cold and repulsive, that it seemed to throw
an icy frigidity through the atmosphere of the room,

and the whole of the guests feeling its chilling influence, sat demure, and dull, and uncomfortable. At
this moment, his Lordship's butler entered the room,
and informed him that he was wanted on urgent business. His lordship immediately rose, and left the com-
pany. At that moment, up started Burns, his generous nature bursting the restraint that had been im-
posed upon it—up he started with a roguish smile on
his face, and in the richest vein of humour, he exclaimed, "Gentlemen, I rise to propose a toast—
here's to his lordship's butler who has been so kind
as to take him away." It scarcely need be added,
that "the feast of reason and the flow of soul" suc-
ceeded this spontaneous outburst from the warm
heart of the bard who had "whistled at the plough."

"The poems of Burns," says an elegant writer,
"grow up like flowers before the tread, they come
like singing birds from the thickets, they grow like
clouds in the sky." Of this character is the poem of
"Tam O'Shanter," the masterpiece of Burns, which
abounds with the happiest strokes of natural humour,
blended with the most beautiful similes, that come
"skelpin' rank and file," as though they had been conceived by the poet with little or no effort. It is said,
that Burns composed this poem in a day—if so, it was
an astonishing performance, and fully verifies the
observation, "that his poems grew like clouds in the
sky."

The broadest strokes, however, of Burns's humour
prevail in his satirical pieces, which for biting sarcasm
have not yet been equalled. Pope, Churchill, and

Byron stand high in the literary world as satirists.
But these distinguished bards invariably weilded the
weapons of their satire in a spirit of rancour and hos-
tility that showed a bad feeling towards those they
attacked. Not so Burns. In a manner peculiar to himself, he points the shafts of his satire with such ironical
humour, though sometimes bordering on vulgarity,
that they doubly effect their purpose. Like a two-edged
sword his satire cuts two ways. While he exposes the
foibles of those he lashes; he, at the same time,
holds them up to ridicule with an unsparing hand ;
and this he, does in the most good humoured style.
Who can read his poem of "*Death and Doctor
Hornbook*," and his other productions of a similar
character, and not admire the quaint and laughter-
provoking humour infused into them ? A rich vein
of humour also pervades his poetical epistles, which
pourtray many pleasing pictures of social friendship
and happiness, and display throughout a complete
Shaksperian knowledge of human character.

These epistles appear to have been written without
any effort, and just according to the mood of mind
the poet was in when he composed them, and though
merely addressed to his rustic friends and associates,
unknown to fame, they rank amongst his happiest
productions.

In his first epistle to "*Davie*," a brother poet,
what a fine social spirit is infused into the following
stanzas :—

" But tent me, Davie, ace of hearts!
    (To say aught less wad wrang the cartes,
        And flatt'ry I detest,)
This life has joys for you and I ;
And joys that riches ne'er could buy ;
    And joys the very best.
There's a' the pleasures o' the heart,
    The lover an' the frien' ;
Ye hae your Meg, your dearest part,
    And I my darling Jean !
        It warms me, it charms me,
            To mention but her name :
        It heats me, it beets me,
            At sets me a' on flame !

All hail, ye tender feelings dear !
The smile of love, the friendly tear,
    The sympathetic glow !
Long since, this world's thorny ways,
Had numbered out my weary days,
    Had it not been for you !
Fate still has blest me with a friend,
    In every care and ill ;
And oft a more endearing band,
    A tie more tender still.
        It lightens, it brightens
            The tenebrific scene,
        To meet with, and greet with
            My Davie or my Jean !"

In Burns's first epistle to "*Lapraik*," another
Scotch bard, how strongly his sociality displays itself
in the following lines :—

" Awa, ye selfish warly race,
    Wha think that havin's, sense an' grace,
    E'en love an' friendship should give place
                    To catch the plack !
    I dinna like to see your face,
                    Nor hear your crack.

But ye whom social pleasure charms,
Whose hearts the tide of kindness warms,
Who hold your being on the terms
    ' Each aid the others,'
Come to my bowl, come to my arms,
    My friends, my brothers."

———

Again, in another epistle to "*Lapraik*," he says,

" O Thou who gies us each guid gift,
Gie me o' wit an' sense a lift,
Then turn me, if Thou please, adrift,
    Through Scotland wide,
Wi' cits nor lairds I wadna shift,
    In a' their pride.

For thus the royal mandate ran,
When first the human race began,
' The social, friendly, honest man,
    Whate'er he be,
'Tis he fulfils great Nature's plan,
    An' none but he !' "

———

Though such the social nature of Burns, though by his power he could throw a charm around the festive board; yet, it is rather singular, that he composed no more than five or six drinking songs. These songs, however, though connected with convivial sentiments, are far superior to the generality of those written on the same subject, especially the song of "*Willie brew'd a peck o' maut*," which forms the next illustration.

This song was composed on the occasion of a "house-warming" given by William Nichol, to which he invited his friends Burns and Allan Masterman, a writing master of Edinbro'. Burns, calling to mind this event, says, "We had such a joyous meeting that Masterman and I agreed, each in his own way, to celebrate the business." The "Willie," therefore, who brewed the malt was William Nichol, the "Allan" who composed the air to the production was Allan Masterman, and he who wrote this choicest of convivial songs was Robert Burns. All three were men of superior genius; but all three, alas, are gone—their heads have long since been laid

> "Under the hillock where the long grass grows."

Professor Wilson, when commenting on the poetry of Burns, says, "You cannot look on this song without crying out, 'O rare Rob Burns!' So far from wishing you to believe that the poet was addicted to drinking, the freshness and fervour of this song convince you that it came out of a healthful heart in the exhiliration of a night that needed not the influence of the flowing bowl." Wordsworth, who was a water drinker, regarded this song with the complacency of a philosopher, knowing well that it is all a pleasant exaggeration, and that "had the moon not lost patience and gone to bed, she would have seen Rob and Allan on their way back to Ellisland, along the bold banks of the Nith, as steady as a brace of bishops!"

Illustration.

O WILLIE BREWED A PECK O' MAUT.

O Willie brewed a peck o' maut,
  And Rob and Allan cam to pree,
Three blyther hearts that lee lang night
  Ye wadna find in Christendie.

" We are nae fou, we're nae that fou !
 But just a drappee in our e'e ;
The cock may craw, the day may daw,
 And aye we'll taste the barley bree."

Here are we met three merry boys,
 Three merry boys, I trow, are we ;
And mony a night we've merry been,
 And mony mae we hope to be.
     " We are not fou, &c.

It is the moon, I ken her horn,
 That's blinkin' in the lift sae hie ;
She shines sae bright to wyle us hame,
 But, by my troth, she'll wait a wee.
     " We are nae fou, &c.

Wha first shall rise to gang awa,
 A cuckold, coward loon is he ;
Wha first beside his chair shall fa',
 He is the king amang us three !
     " We are nae fou, &c.

As we advance in the pilgrimage of life how frequently, with a feeling of pleasure, we recal sweet
memories of the past—how frequently, before our
mental vision, we bring the scenes of our early years,
the companions of our former days, the happy hours
departed never to return, which once we enjoyed before becoming acquainted with the anxieties and cares
of a more matured stage of existence. This feeling,
no doubt, the sensitive heart of Burns felt when he
conceived the idea of composing the most popular
social song in our language. We allude to the song
of "*Auld Lang Syne*," which embodying sentiments,

as it does, so deeply connected with our best affections, will for ever retain its popularity.

Burns, in a letter to his esteemed friend, Mrs. Dunlop, says, "Is not the Scotch phrase, 'Auld lang syne,' exceedingly expressive? There is an old song and tune bears this name which has often thrilled through my soul. Light be the turf on the breast of the heaven-inspired poet who composed this glorious fragment." In communicating this song to his publisher, he further remarked, "The following song, an old song of the olden times, and which I have never seen in print, not even in manuscript, until I took it down from an old man's singing, is enough to recommend any air." Allan Cunningham, however, the eminent biographer of Burns, says, "These are strong words; but there can be no doubt that, save for a line or two, we owe this song, *to no other minstrel, than minstrel, Burns.*"

—

Illustration.

AULD LANG SYNE.

Should auld acquaintance be forgot
　And never brought to min,
Should auld acquaintance be forgot,
　And days o' lang syne.
　　　　For auld lang syne, my dear,
　　　　　For auld lang syne,
　　　　We'll tak a cup o' kindness yet,
　　　　　For auld lang syne.

We twa hae run about the braes
　And pou't the gowans fine;
But we've wandered mony a weary foot
　Sin auld lang syne.
　　　　For auld lang syne, &c.

We twa hae paidl't i' the burn,
  Frae mornin' sun till dine :
But seas between us braid hae roar'd,
  Sin auld lang syne.
      For auld lang syne, &c.

And here's a hand, my trusty fiere,
  And gie's a hand o' thine ;
And we'll tak a right guid willie-waught,
  For auld lang syne !
      For auld lang syne, &c.

And surely ye'll be your pint-stowp,
  And surely I'll be mine ;
And we'll tak a cup o' kindness yet,
  For auld lang syne.
      For auld lang syne, my dear,
        For auld lang syne,
      We'll tak a cup o' kindness yet,
        For auld lang syne !

CHAPTER X.

The Influence of Woman on Burns as a poet.

It is said that Burns, like all men of high sentiment, never loved fully but once. It was the beauty
of Mary Campbell that so strongly awakened in his
heart the master passion of his nature, Love, and his
love for her was pure as it was ardent. The inten-
sity of this love he subsequently diffused through the
whole of his beautiful love songs, which breathe the
very spirit of tenderness. In them he has exalted the
character of woman more than any other poet. With
the skill of a master he has alike painted the beauty of
her mind and the graces of her person, in strains

varied with "the sweetest hues of expression and the highest turns of thought." Never did poet kneel at the shrine of female loveliness with more devotion— never did poet offer sweeter incense at this shrine, nor wear Love's fetters with a more willing heart than Robert Burns. Other poets in praise of woman may have sung in more lofty strains, but none with more power and sweetness. He worshipped the pure and beautiful in nature; but, of all God's creations, he worshipped woman most. Within his own heart he strongly felt the witchery of her charms, the magic power of her influence, and most truthfully he described what he felt.

To show the influence of the gentler sex, Campbell, in his "Pleasures of Hope," thus praises woman :—

> " Without the smile by partial beauty won
>   O what were man ?—a world without a sun !"

And again how highly he praises her in the following couplet :—

> " The world was sad, the garden bloomed a wild,
>   And man, the hermit, sighed till woman smiled."

But what are the sentiments of Burns on the same subject? He gives utterance to them as though a thrill of transport shot through his veins, as though his heart was proud to acknowledge the great ascendency which woman's beauty had over it. "O woman," he exclaims, " Nature's darling child,"

> " Not the poet, in the moment
>   Fancy lightens in his e'e,
>   Kens the pleasure, feels the rapture
>   That thy presence gi'es to me !"

And then, as though past delights came rushing into his mind, he exclaims

> " The sweetest hours that I ever spend
> Are spent amang the lasses O !"

And with the same feeling he thus gives utterance to the following truthful lines :—

> " What signifies the life o' man
> And 'twere na for the lasses O !"

The fact is, Woman was the inspiring muse of Burns. It was her beauty that first awoke the poetic impulse within him. It was the witchery of her charms that enkindled the finer sensibilities of his nature to adore her. In describing her beauty, her form, and her mind, he gave expression to the most pure, the most exalted sentiments. From the material imagery around him he produced the sweetest poetic similes to depict the graces of her person and the purity of her mind. He compared her charms to every thing beautiful in nature. When he wrote the image of woman appeared to dwell in his mind. " He wrote," Allan Cunningham says, " as though her eye was always upon him."

> " *He saw her* in the dewy flowers,
> *He saw her* sweet and fair,
> *He heard her* in the tunefu' birds,
> *He heard her* charm the air."

" Rapture-giving woman," was to him

> " The gust o' joy, the balm o' woe,
> The soul o' life, the heaven below."

And speaking on this subject, in one of his poems, he himself humorously acknowledges that

".There's a' wee faut they whiles lay to me,
  I like the lasses, Gude forgie me !"

But the best record connected with this subject is
the following happy effusion :—

—

Illustration.

THERE'S NOUGHT BUT CARE.

CHORUS.

Green grow the rashes, O !
  Green grow the rashes, O !
The sweetest hours that I e'er spend
  Are spent amang the lasses, O.

There's nought but care on ev'ry han',
  In every hour that passes, O :
What signifies the life o' man,
  An' 'twere na for the lasses, O.

The warly race may riches chase,
  An' riches still may fly them, O ;
An' tho' at last they catch them fast,
  Their hearts can ne'er enjoy them, O.

But gie me a canny hour at e'en,
  My arms about my dearie, O ;
An' warly cares, an' warly men,
  May a' gae tapsalteerie, O.

For you sae douce, ye sneer at this,
  Ye're nought but senseless asses, O :
The wisest man the warl' e'er saw,
  He dearly lov'd the lasses, O.

Auld Nature swears the lovely dears
  Her noblest work she classess, O,
Her 'prentice han' she try'd on man,
  An' then she made the lasses, O.

      Green grow, &c.

This song is worth a hundred dull homilies in praise of woman. While Burns thus elevates the fair sex he shows his admiration of them. In a letter to Thomson, his publisher, he says, " Whenever I want to be more than ordinary in song, I put myself in the regimen of admiring a fine woman, and proportion to the adorability of her charms, in proportion you are delighted with my verses. The lightning of her eye is the godhead of Parnassus, and the witchery of her smiles the divinity of Helicon." One of his happiest productions, " *John Anderson, my jo,*" forms an exception to this rule. This composition displays no impassioned strains that evince the " pulse's maddening play," no thrilling relation of a lover's transports "amang the rigs o' barley," nor yet the " heart-felt rapture" of a

> " Youthful, happy pair,
> In other's arms, breathing out the tender tale
> Beneath the milk-white thorn that scents the evening gale."

But he presents to us a picture of a happy pair, enjoying domestic peace and happiness, even in the decline of life, by

> " The blink o' *their* ain fireside."

In fancy we behold " John Anderson" and his aged partner seated together, bringing to recollection the " days o' lang syne." John we may imagine, who was once so trim from " tap to toe," still looks fresh and hale as an ancient oak, though seventy summers have passed over his head. Thus seated, we may conceive how wistfully his old dame surveys his features, as

fondly she brings to mind the happy time when they
were " first acquent," the time when his "locks were
like the raven," and his " bonnie brow was brent."
On hearing these words we may fancy how the old
man's face mantles with a smile. In tender strain
she then continues—

> " But now your brow is bald, John,
> Your locks are like the snaw,
> But blessings on your frosty pow,
> John Anderson, my jo."

In the next stanza she again reverts to the past.
She reminds him of the time when they " clamb the
hill thegither" and of the " canty days" they had enjoyed, and then serenely looking through the vista of
the future, she thus gives expression to her feelings :

> " We now maun totter down, John,
> But hand in hand we'll go—"

And then, as though even Death itself should not
part them, she tenderly adds—

> " We'll sleep thegither at the foot,
> John Anderson, my jo."

No lyric in our language surpasses this in beauty
and tenderness.   Every word, every sentiment it
breathes, bears the impress of Burns's genius, and
like an evergreen in the variegated garden of Poesy
it will ever retain its freshness and fragrance.

Illustration.

JOHN ANDERSON.

John Anderson my jo, John,
 When we were first acquent ;
Your locks were like the raven,
 Your bonnie brow was brent ;
But now your brow is beld, John,
 Your locks are like the snaw ;
But blessings on your frosty pow,
 John Anderson my jo.

John Anderson my jo, John,
 We clamb the hill thegither ;
And mony a canty day, John,
 We've had wi' ane anither :
Now we maun totter down, John,
 But hand in hand we'll go ;
And sleep thegither at the foot,
 John Anderson my jo.

In praise of woman Burns is considered the most truthful of all poets. Her beauty is the Alpha and Omega of his poems. The influence which her attractions had on his heart pervades the greater part of them. When he was "beardless, young, and blate," as he himself expressed, it was the beauty of a bewitching girl, his partner in the harvest field, that first awoke in his breast the emotions of Love. Alluding to this, in one of his poems, he exclaims,

" I see her yet, the sonsie queen,
 That lighted up my jingle,
 Her witching smile, her pauky e'en,
 That gart my heart-strings tingle."

It was in praise of this "sonsic queen," with her "witching smile," that he first struck his rustic harp, whose strings he afterwards swept with such wonderful power and sweetness, and which he swept for the last time when he composed the following song in honour of Miss Charlotte Hamilton, the maid of Devon :—

Illustration.

FAIREST MAID ON DEVON BANKS.

Fairest maid on Devon banks,
    Crystal Devon, winding Devon,
Wilt thou lay that frown aside,
    And smile as thou were wont to do ?
Full well thou know'st I love thee, dear !
Could't thou to malice lend an ear?
O ! did not love exclaim " Forbear,
    Nor use a faithful lover so."

Then come, thou fairest of the fair,
Those wonted smiles O let me share,
And by beauteous self I swear,
    No love but thine my heart shall know,
    Fairest maid on Devon banks,
        Crystal Devon, winding Devon,
    Wilt thou lay that frown aside,
        And smile as thou were wont to do !

These stanzas were the last that Burns produced. He composed them only a few days before his death, as his thoughts reverted to early days. His once robust frame was then emaciated, his hopes were fled, his prospects blighted, and his heart, as he said, was "weak as a woman's tear," at the thought of leaving

his wife, then near confinement, and his four children helpless orphans. Speaking on this subject,
in a letter to a friend, he says, "Alas, my friend, I
fear the voice of the bard will never be heard among
you any more. You actually would not know me if
you saw me. Pale, emaciated, and so feeble, as occasionally to need help from a chair. And the worst
of the matter is this : when an exciseman is off duty,
his salary is reduced to £35 instead of £50. What
way, in the name of thrift, shall I maintain myself,
and keep a horse in country quarters, with a wife and
five children, on £35. I mention this, because I had
intended to beg your utmost interest, and that of all
the friends you can muster, to move our commis-
sioners of excise to grant me the full salary ; I dare
say you know them personally. If they do not grant
it me, I must lay my account with an exit truly *en
poëte ;* if I die not of disease, I must perish with
hunger."

What sad forebodings were these to "Scotland's
proudly-gifted peasant son," the man who was an
honour to her, and who had been feasted and idolised
at the tables of her nobility. Poor Burns, the brightest
genius Scotland ever produced, the greatest man of
the age in which he lived, was afraid—yes, we have
his own words for it—was afraid of *perishing with
hunger!* How cheerless, how pitiable, alas, must then
have been his condition! Yet for all this the manly
spirit of Burns never sank, his fortitude never gave
way ; but, as the sand of his existence was rapidly
running out, his genius, triumphing over the pressure

of poverty and the loss of strength, shone, to the very
last, in all its glorious brightness, until at length
"stern Ruin's plough-share" crushed him "beneath
the furrow's weight," and his melodious harp became
silent for ever.

> "Mourn, guilty Scotland, mourn!
> Bow to the dust in widow'd shame—
> Hide thee in sackcloth, with dishevelled hair:
> But wreathe around the urn of Burns
> No mournful yew—the laughing thorn, his claim,
> Twined with harebell and daisy let him wear."

CHAPTER XI.

On the Nationality and Independence of Burns.

If there is one thing which distinguishes the
people of Scotland more than any other people
in the world it is their nationality. An ardent
attachment to his native land, and to every thing
associated with it, is a feeling which

> " Grows with the growth, and strengthens with the strength"

Of every true son of Caledonia. This feeling takes
deep root in his heart, he loves to cherish it wherever
he moves and has his being. When far away in a
distant land how often the well-known carols of Burns
beguiles his time and recals

> " The scenes that blessed him when a child,"

And his heart, dwelling on the past,

> " Glows and gladdens at the charms
> Of Scotia's woods and waterfalls."

The popular ballad of "*Annie Laurie*" was the favorite ditty of our Highland regiments when serving in the Crimea. These kilted warriors frequently beguiled the tedious hours there by singing this ballad. They sang it on the tented field as well as in the midnight trenches before Sebastopol, as their thoughts probably reverted to their beloved country and its dear associations, for whether at home or abroad these regiments never lose their nationality—

> " Wherever they wander, wherever they rove,
> The hills of the highlands they dearly love."

And such was the feeling that burned in the breast of Burns. Scotland never produced a man who had this feeling more intensely in his nature. Burns was a Scotchman to the backbone. His heart was in his country. His soul idolized every thing that belonged to it. His love for her is photographed in his poems. The scenes he describes in them are all entirely Scottish. His Muse, in no single instance, ever sought foreign lands for a subject. His nationality, therefore, shines conspicuously throughout the whole of his productions. He was proud of the Scottish name, and he gloried in being a Scotchman. No man could be more proud of the country that gave him birth. He was proud of her ancient heroes, of her heroic achievements, and her glorious struggles to maintain her independence. He loved to pay homage

to her departed minstrels, he loved her music, her
"bonnie banks and braes," her heather-clad mountains, and every thing which added to her glory, to
her honour, and to her happiness as a nation. It was
this love that prompted him to turn "the weeder
clips aside," and spare the "rough burr thistle" for
the symbol's sake. It was this love that bound his
very soul to Scotland. and gave immortality to his
compositions ; for

> " Dear to him was Scotland,
> In her sons and in her daughters,
> In her Highlands—Lowlands—Islands.
> Regal woods and rushing waters :
> In the glory of her story
> When her tartans fired the field !
> Scotland ! oft betrayed—beleagur'd—
> Scotland ! never known to yield !
> Dear to him her Doric language,
> Thrill'd his heart-strings at her name,
> And he left her more than rubies
> In the riches of his fame !"

The nationality of Burns was never more strongly
evinced than when he first passed from Scottish on
to English ground. Immediately on doing this, he
threw off his hat, and kneeling down and looking
towards Scotland, he thus, with uplifted hands,
solemnly exclaimed—

> " O Scotia ! my dear, my native soil !
>   For whom my warmest wish to heaven is sent !
> Long may thy hardy sons of rustic toil,
>   Be blest with health, and peace, and sweet content !
> And O ! may heaven their simple lives prevent

From luxury's contagion, weak and vile!
Then, howe'er crowns and coronets be rent,
A virtuous populace may rise the while,
And stand a wall of fire around their much lov'd Isle."

In the moment of enthusiastic ardour, and in this romantic manner, did Burns, with his patriotic heart, evince his love for old Scotia and her "hardy sons of russet toil" for whom he breathed this prayer, so truly noble and poetical. How beautiful and full of nationality is the following production :—

Illustration.

CALEDONIA.

Their groves o' sweet myrtle let foreign lands reckon,
  Where bright-beaming summers exalt the perfume;
Far dearer to me yon lone glen o' green breckan,
  Wi' the burn stealing under the lang yellow broom:
Far dearer to me are yon humble broom bowers,
  Where the blue-bell and gowan lurk lowly unseen;
For there, lightly tripping amang the wild flowers,
  A listening the linnet, aft wanders my Jean.

Tho' rich is the breeze in their gay sunny valleys,
  And cauld Caledonia's blast on the wave;
Their sweet-scented woodlands that skirt the proud palace,
  What are they?—The haunt of the tyrant and slave!
The slave's spicy forests, and gold-bubbling fountains,
  The brave Caledonian views wi' disdain;
He wanders as free as the winds of his mountains,
  Save love's willing fetters, the chains o' his Jean.

We shall now turn to the independence of Burns, a quality he possessed to so remarkable a degree as

appeared at times to border on extravagance. It is said
that no man ever prided himself more on the independence of his character.

In dedicating his poems to the noblemen and
gentlemen of the Caledonian Hunt, he says, "Though
much indebted to your goodness, I do not approach
you, my Lords and gentlemen, in the usual style of
dedication, to thank you for past favours ; that path
is so hacknied by prostituted learning that honest
rusticity is ashamed of it.   Nor do I present this address with the venal soul of a servile author, looking
for a continuation of these favours.   *I was bred to
the plough, and am independent.*"   Thus spake the
brave heart of Burns—" I was bred to the plough,
and am independent."   His soul disdained cringing
to obtain mercenary favours—his heart scorned to
prostitute his genius by fulsome adoration—his spirit
soared above such degradation.   Burns was a man,
and despised lowering the dignity of his manhood.
He looked on all men as " brothers of the earth," no
matter what position they occupied.   He believed,
and he was correct in his belief, that

> " Worth makes the man, the want of it the fellow,
>   The rest is all but leather and prunella,"

And that it is

> " Man's inhumanity to man,
>   Makes the countless thousands mourn."

In one of his letters to a friend, Burns, when
speaking on this subject, says, " What signify the
silly, idle gewgaws of wealth, or the ideal trumpery

of greatness. When fellow partakers of the same
nature fear the same God, have the same benevolence
of heart; the same nobleness of soul, the same detes-
tation of every thing dishonest, and the same scorn
of every thing unworthy; if they are not in the de-
pendance of absolute beggary, in the name of common sense are they not equals? And if the bias, the
instinctive bias of their souls were the same way, why
may they not be friends? These were the thoughts of
Burns. He was the poet of Independence. His poems,
therefore, contain no servile ideas.

> " Nurst in the peasant's lowly shed,
> · To hardy independence bravely bred,

He scorned to be " the servile, mercenary Swiss of
Rhymes." Rather than my character should be thus
branded, he indignantly exclaims, in a poetical epistle
to Robert Graham, Esq., let

> " My horny fist assume the plough again ;
> The pie-bald jacket let me patch once more ;
> · On eighteen pence a week I've lived before."

But though his race on earth was brief, though the
path he trod was dark, and though " hungry ruin"
too often " had him in the wind ;" yet

> " He kept his honesty and truth,
>   His independent tongue and pen,
> And moved in manhood and in youth,
>   Pride of his fellow men.
>
> Strong sense, deep feeling, passions strong,
>   A hate of tyrant, and of knave,
> A love of right, a scorn of wrong.
>   Of coward and of slave ;

A kind true heart, a spirit high,
  That could not fear, that could not bow,
Were written in his manly eye,
  And on his manly brow."

The noblest Ode to Independence in our language is " *A man's a man for a' that.*" Burns believed
that this production contained " two or three good
thoughts inverted into rhyme." Every verse, however, of this poem glows with gems from the mine
of Truth, and shows that in intelligence and extended views of humanity Burns was a century in
advance of the age in which he lived. In this effusion, which will live while there is a spirit of independence in the heart of man, he scans, with the eye
of a seer, the vista of the future, and prophecies the
" Good time coming," when

" Sense and worth o'er a' the earth
  May bear the gree and a' that;
For a' that and a' that,
  Its coming yet for a' that.
That man to man the warld o'er
  Shall brothers be for a' that."

CHAPTER XII.

Concluding Remarks.

The great soul of Burns quitted its mortal frame
in the morning of the 25th of July, 1797, in the
thirty-seventh year of his age. Though he died in
extreme poverty, yet he owed no one a shilling.

When looking back on his brief, eventful career, how much we find to admire, how much to pity and censure. He had his faults, he had his failings; but who is there in these respects that is blameless? While we learn, then, to profit by avoiding his failings, let us cherish in remembrance his virtues, and do honour to one who weighed the "inborn worth of man," and made

> " Rustic life and poverty
> Grow beautiful beneath his touch."

That Burns had many failings he himself in his poems frequently admits with sorrow; but, it is now generally acknowledged that they have been much, very much exaggerated. The greatest of his failings was want of prudence in managing his own affairs. But whatever they were, the noble qualities of his nature shone out like bright stars in his character. These qualities were a glorious intellect, a magnanimous moral nature, a strong religious element within him, a generous manly heart, and an honourable mind that scorned to commit a mean and selfish action. But it is boldly asserted by some that Burns with all his intellectual endowments was at best little else than an habitual drunkard. Those who go so far as to assert this, cannot, we think, possess a general knowledge of his character and writings. Mr. Findlater, many years superintendent of Burns as an excise officer, when defending his character against the base aspersions then cast upon it, says, "I have seen Burns in all his various phases—in his convivial moments, in his sober moods, and in the bosom of his family, and I never beheld any thing like the gross enormities with which he has been charged—with his family, I will venture to say, he *never was seen otherwise than as attentive and affectionate in a high degree.*" This we believe to be the case, for during the latter part of his life at Dumfries, how did he employ himself? Most assuredly not like a drunkard. A great portion of his time he spent in educating his sons in the rudiments of knowledge—he was editing, at the same time, a new edition of his works, corresponding daily with the most distinguished ladies and learned men of Scotland—writing the best songs ever penned, and sending them gratuitously by dozens for insertion in Thomson's Musical Museum— and moreover discharging, in an exemplary manner, the onerous duties of an exciseman, in which occupation he was in the habit of riding two hundred miles a week! What man, we ask, doing so great an amount of mental and bodily labour could be a drunkard? The question requires no answer. But the fame of Burns has outlived the malice of his calumniators. His worth as a man has risen in public estimation, and his renown as a poet has extended to all parts of the globe.

How strongly, how universally was this manifested on the memorable twenty-fifth of January, 1859, when the centenary of his birth was so enthusiastically celebrated. With one generous impulse, wherever the English language was spoken, thousands and tens of thousands then met to do homage to his memory. Never before was poet so honoured. The mightiest potentate, the greatest conqueror never received so general and so warm-hearted an ovation. Well might the two sons of Burns as they sat that day at the banquet of glory with the nobles and literati of Scotland—well might they be proud of their illustrious father, and rejoice to think that justice had at last been accorded to his worth and genius. At the glorious gatherings in celebration of this day the failings of the bard were all forgotten—his virtues and poetic power only remembered—and now, looking at the bright side of his character, it may truly be said, that "Take him for all in all he was one of the noblest specimens of humanity."

Burns was a member of the Dumfries volunteers when he died; he was, therefore, buried with all the pomp of military honours. The late Allan Cunningham, who was an eye-witness of the funeral, beautifully observes, in his life of Burns, that "all the military array of foot and horse did not harmonise either with the genius or the fortunes of the poet, and that the tears which he saw on many cheeks around, as the earth was replaced, were worth all the splendour of a show which mocked with unintended mockery the burial of the poor and neglected Burns."

"As a poet," says Professor Wilson, "he may be placed amongst the highest order of human beings who have benefitted their race by the expressions of noble sentiment and glorious thoughts. From his inexhaustible fancy, warmed by the sunshine of his own heart, he strewed along the weary ways of the world flowers so beautiful that even to eyes that

weep—that are familiar with tears—they look as if
they were flowers dropped from heaven.   Burns is
the poet of the people.   They loved him when living,
they mourned for him when dead. They felt that they
had lost their greatest man, and it is no exaggeration
to say, that Scotland was saddened on the day of his
funeral.   It is seldom that tears are ever shed close
to the grave beyond the inner circle that narrows it
round, but that day there were tears in the eyes of
many far off at work, and that night there was silence
in thousands of cottages that had so often heard his
songs."

> " Farewell, high chief of Scottish song !
>   That couldst alternately impart
>   Wisdom and rapture in thy page,
>   And brand each vice with satire strong,
>   Whose lines are mottoes of the heart,
>   Whose truths electrify the sage.
>
>   Farewell, and ne'er may Envy dare
>   To wing one baleful poison drop
>   From the crushed laurels of thy bust ;
>   But while the lark sings sweet in air,
>   Still may the grateful pilgrim stop,
>   To bless the spot that holds thy dust."

LINES TO THE MEMORY OF BURNS,

BY THE AUTHOR.

And spoken by him at the Stockton Centenary Dinner in honour of Burns.

———

Soul of th' immortal Burns! old Scotia's pride!
" Who walked in glory by the mountain's side,"
Where Coila found thee, by thy numbers led,
And smiling bound the holly round thy head!
O soul of Burns! to whom was kindly given,
Th' inspired light that only comes from heaven,
This night, to honour thee, we come not here,
T" embalm thy memory with a trickling tear ;
But come with social hearts, in revelry,
To spend, sweet bard, a mental hour with thee,
And celebrate with songs thy natal day,
After one hundred years have rolled away.

Time was, when Feeling fled the tuneful throng,
When mawkish verse usurped the realms of Song,
And babbling poets sang in senseless strains
Of love-sick shepherds on Arcadian plains,
Where every Strephon, when his Phœbe frowned,
Made all the rocks with Phœbe's name resound :
But BURNS arose, and scanning Nature's page,
He spurned the puling ditties of the age ;
Truth for his polar star, he seized the lyre,
And once more gave us sparks of Nature's fire !
Whate'er his theme, so varied were his powers,
He beautified it with poetic flowers
In manly verse—his constant, dearest plan
To raise the inborn dignity of man,
To teach with lessons sage all human kind,
And Independence plant in every mind.

How sweet his song when Love inspired the strain,
How broad his Humour when in happy vein,
How keen his Satire, how each arrow hit,
Pointed with withering Ridicule and Wit !
What Wisdom shines in " man was made to mourn,"
How grand the battle Ode of Bannock-burn,
Where every thought defies a tyrant's aim,
And every marshalled word is winged with flame !

O Scotland, Queen of Song ! to Burns so dear,
Well may thy hardy sons his name revere,
And love the Land that could in him give birth
To so much genius, sense, and sterling worth ;
For States may fade, and Empires fall by turns,
Ere Nature moulds again another Burns.

Farewell, dear bard ! sweet lyrist of the heart !
High priest of Song, that can rich joys impart !
While Truth and Nature have the power to charm,
While Love can prompt a passion pure and warm,
And Scottish breasts with Scotland's deeds are fired,
Thy matchless lays will live and be admired !

Farewell, sweet bard, who mourned the daisy's fate,
And in thy bloom fell 'neath the furrow's weight ;
Though this thy lot, yet still in every clime,
As ages hasten down the steep of Time,
Allied to genius will descend thy name,
The best and sweetest lyrist on the page of Fame.

LIST OF SUBSCRIBERS.

STOCKTON.

Mr. John Alderson, Messrs. Faber & Wilson's office
Mr. John Alderson, goods manager
Mr. George Allan, painter
Mr. William Allan, collector
Mr. John Addinell

Edward D'Oyley Bayley, Esq.
Mr. John Barker, auctioneer
Mr. George Barnes, clerk
Mr. Frederick Bell, chemist
Mr. James Bell, pork dealer
Mr. F. J. H. Bellringer, clerk
Mr. G. Y. Blair, engineer
Mr. Thomas Bowron, builder
Mr. J. B. Robson, Mr. Dodds's office
Mr. C. S. Booth, hosier
Mr. James Brown, iron founder
Mr. John Brotherton, clerk
Mr. William Bolam, professor of music
Mr. A. Brittain, clerk, 2 copies
Joshua Byers, Esq.

Mr. Miles Cadle, ironmonger
Mr. William Clephan, joiner
Mr. John Clephan, grocer
Mr. Robert Clennett, painter
Mr. Samuel Crummack, fitter

Mr. John Dent, joiner
Mr. T. P. Dickenson, Jun., clerk
Mr. John Danby, commercial traveller, 2 copies

P

Mr. Lampson Eden, hair dresser

John Farquharson, Esq., surgeon
Mr. Henry Fawcus, timber merchant
Wm. Foss, Esq., surgeon
Mrs. Foulstone
Mr. John Fowler, engineer

Mr. Gear, painter

Mr. R. T. Hall, timber merchant. 2 copies
  ,,   James Heald, 3, Nelson-street
  ,,   John Hind, Jun., plumber
  ,,   Thomas Hind, printer
  ,,   T. W. Hornsby, auctioneer
  ,,   Robert Higgenbottam, tinner

Mr. Aleck Iley, joiner
  ,,   J. P. Jewson, music dealer
  ,,   R. J. Jackson, currier
  ,,   Jones, hatter

Mr. Ketton, miller
  ,,   Charles Kirton, Gazette Office

Mr. Henry Linton, joiner
  ,,   Robert Lowe, 101, High-street

Mr. John Maddison, brass founder
  ,,   Robert Maw, draper
  ,,   R. T. Mellanby, grocer
Miss Ann Mellanby
Mr. John Miller, contractor
Mrs. Moses, George inn

Mr. George Manners, publican, 2 copies
  ,,   William Marshall, harbour master
  ,,   Thomas Nelson, builder
  ,,   J. Noad, engraver

Richard Ord, Esq., 2 copies

Mr. Patterson, reporter " Darlington Times"
  ,,   Johnson Pickering, saddler

Mrs. Plews
Mr. John Porter, publican

Mr. Robert Taylor Rand, clerk
  ,, George Raine, milk dealer, 2 copies
William Richardson, Esq., surgeon, 2 copies
Thomas Richmond, Esq.
Mr. Thomas Richlieu, tailor
  ,, Abel Roberts, publican
  ,, Thomas Rose, engineman
  ,, William Robinson, clerk
  ,, Thomas Robinson, grocer
  ,, Routledge, Messrs. Close & Co.'s Office
  ,, Rose, joiner, 2 copies

The Rev. Robert Spears
Mr. J. A. Sanders, druggist, 2 copies
  ,, Henry Sanderson, saddler
  ,, William Scaife, tailor
  ,, William Sharp, clerk
  ., William Smith, fitter
  ,, W. D. Smith, upholsterer
  ,, Thomas Swenson, Bishopton Lane
  ,, John Simpson, middle-street
William Simpson, Esq., wine merchant, 2 copies

Mr. Robert Taylor, clerk
  ,, J. G. Thompson, solicitor
Charles Trotter, Esq., 2 copies

Mr. William Walton, Sen., earthenware dealer
  ,, Thomas Walton, Stockton Saw Mill
  ,, Young Walton,   do.   2 copies
  ,, W. J. Watson, clerk
John Hansell Wren, Esq., 2 copies
Thomas Wren, Jun., Esq., 2 copies
Mr. J. W. Wilson, painter
  ,, Francis Wetherall, joiner
Robert Corney Weatherill, Esq.
Mr. Thomas Woolman, bookbinder, 2 copies
  ,, Byron Webber, reporter, 2 copies
  ., William Wilson, tailor

SOUTH STOCKTON.

Mr. James Bowron, bottle works
,, B. R. Smith, tallow chandler
,, John Whalley, pottery
Mr. William Wise, Saw Mill, 2 copies

DURHAM.

Mr. John Reed Appleton, F. S. A., Western hill,
    10 copies
,, Charles Ashton, New North Road
,, George Gradon, Western hill
,, William Hutchinson, Western hill
,, John Morton, 2, South-street
,, Henry Reaveley, 10, Elvet Bridge
,, William Shadforth, New North Road
,, Samuel Richardson Vann, 3, Saddler-street
,, Charles Felgate White, 1, Saddler-street
,, Thomas Thompson

NEWCASTLE.

Mr. J. H. Bell, 22, Blandford-street
A. H. Burdo, Esq.
Mr. John Brewis, 28, Groat Market
Miss A. Cleugh, Wesley Terrace
Mr. J. Cochrane, Sunderland-street
,, John Chattaway, decorative artist
,, Cuthbert Edwards
,, J. W. Fletcher
,, J. Greener
Henry Gilpin, Esq. author of the "Massacre of the
    Bards and other Poems"
W. W. Smith, Esq.
J. Harrison, Esq.
Mr. Henry Hayton, Wesley Terrace
,, Alexander Nevins
,, William Robson
W. Ross, Esq., Blandford-street
W. W. Smith, Esq.
Mr. William Simpson

Mr. John Waters, Wellington Hotel
Miss Barbara Weddell
,, Alice Weddell

NORTON.

John Hogg, Esq.
Charles Swain, Esq.
Mr. John Wilkinson
,, R. P. Seymour
,, R. Richardson, porter merchant

YARM.

George Williams, Esq., solicitor
Mr. Joseph Ramsey

MIDDLESBRO.

Mr. J. A. Anderson
Burns's Literary and Benevolent Club
Mr. Charles Bell, draper
,, William Burnett
,, Richard Coates
,, James Cawthorn
,, James Duncan
,, Thomas Davies
Edward Gilkes, Esq.
Mr. William Gillespie
,, William Garbutt, Jun.
,, Alexander Johnson
,, Thomas Lincoln
,, James Miller
,, Richard Potter
,, W. Petchell
,, W. Surridge
,, William Saite
,, Thomas Sanderson
,, John Taylor

HARTLEPOOL.

Mr. John Procter, bookseller, 2 copies

Mr. Jon. Garbutt
,, J. E. Robson
,, C. Hoggett
,, A. S. Orton, Reporter "Hartlepool Mercury

WEST HARTLEPOOL.

Mr. Dalziel, dyer, 12 copies
,, T. J. Taylor, music teacher
Miss Watson, Arches-street

DARLINGTON.

Mr. Thomas Watson, author of the "Ruin and other Poems," 2 copies
Mr. Thomas Turner, King's Head inn
,, John Thomas Abbott, Rose Villa
,, Anthony Dinsdale
,, William Watson
,, Richard Benson
,, Andrew Common
,, E. P. Elgie
,, George Brigham
,, Nicholas Bragg
,, John Bousfield
,, Thomas Robinson

ESCRICK PARK, Yorkshire.

Mr. C. Abbott, 2 copies
Mrs. Chambers

ALFRETON, DERBYSHIRE.

Mr. Richard Burbeck, railway works
,, James Cox, railway works
,, Samual Rowbottom, stationer
,, James Rowbottom, ironmonger
,, George Siddell, surgeon
,, Joseph Siddell, assistant surgeon
,, Alexander Smith, railway works
,, John Smith, Croft Head, Kinniemiar, Scotland

Miss Isabella Smith, Devonrove, Scotland
Mr. Alexander Wilton, iron works, 2 copies

WINDERMERE, CUMBERLAND.

Miss Sarah Burgess, Storrs Hall, 2 copies
Mr. Hecsom, Storrs Hall

GAINFORD.

Mr. Bowman, Gainford Academy, 12 copies
Miss Jane Hardy

LEITH.

Mr. John James Lundy, F. G. S. Primrose Bank
Mrs. J. J. Lundy, do.

EDINBRO'.

Mrs. Young, Fountain Bridge
Mary Ann Young, do.

MANCHESTER.

Mr. Joseph Hutton, bookbinder, Manchester
,, Isaac Bowes, accountant, Manchester
Miss S. A. Higgenbottam, Walkden School House,
    Worsley, near Manchester

STOKESLEY.

Mr. George Tweddell, author of "Shakspere and his
    contemporaries"
Master George Tweddell, painter

LEEDS.

Mr. J. T. Beer, Briggate, Leeds
,, William Garland, North-street

VARIOUS PLACES.

Mr. Adkinson, civil engineer, Era Place, Soung lane, Battersea, London, 2 copies

„ Edwin Avery, Trafalgar Cottage, Cheltenham, 6 copies

„ William Bowkett, Hop Market Hotel, Worcester

Mrs. Briggs, Bishopton

Mr. Edward Capern, author of "Songs and Ballads," Bideford, Devonshire

„ John Forster, draper, Barnardcastle

Frederick Hill, Esq., Birmingham

Mr. John Anthony Benson, Portrack House

Miss Lucy Lovell, Naferton, near Driffield

Mr. Johnson, Temperance advocate, Middleton-one-Row

„ William Parker, Percy-street, Hull

Mr. Parkin, Prospect Terrace, Dronfield, near Sheffield, Yorkshire

Mrs. Parkin, do.

Messrs. Parsons, Fletcher, & Co. Bread-street, London

Mr. William Reynolds, East-street, London Road, Leicester

„ Thomas Simpson, 12, Holmside, Sunderland 5 copies

Miss Spencer, Lough Rews, Ireland

Mrs. Simpson, Petersham, near Richmond, Surrey

Mr. Harwood Simpson, Stratford, Essex

Master H. H. Simpson, do.

Mr. Robert Sanderson, tailor, Kildale, Yorkshire

Joseph Wren, Esq. Boston, 2 copies

Mr. David Wilson Barker, Melksham, Wiltshire

„ Alfred Watt, Guisbro'

HENRY HEAVISIDES, PRINTER, STOCKTON.

THE PLEASURES OF HOME
AND OTHER POEMS.
THIRD EDITION.

BY HENRY HEAVISIDES.

Opinions of the Press, &c. on the Work.

" The volume before us is from the press as well as the pen of
Mr. Henry Heavisides, of Stockton, and we have pleasure in
noticing the fact that as a product of the typographer's art, it is as
commendable a production as are its literary beauties honorable
to the author's taste and genius. No one can read the productions
of his pen without recognising poetic beauties of a high character,
and acknowledging the presence of great moral as well as imaginative power."—*Hartlepool Mercury.*

" Mr. Heavisides "twangs the homely lyre" most musically, and
proves himself an earnest-minded, warm-hearted, and cheerful
poet of the hearth. His thoughts are manly, generous, and well-
expressed. The occasional indulgence of a humorous vein brings
out another amiable trait of the poet's character, and gives to his
verse the charm of variety. The "Pleasures of Home" is a book
worthy of any table, and printed as a good book should be."—
Darlington Times.

" The Pleasures of Home contains some very gentle scenes and
touching features, more particularly those parts which are drawn
from the poet's own heart and copied from his own observations. Other bards have showered more bitter execrations
on conquerors and despots, but few have sung with truer
knowledge, or in more moving strains, the sweets of the domestic
hearth or of the faces that gladden it."—*Allan Cunningham.*

" The muse of Mr. Heavisides is from the flowery region of
Parnassus—she has drank at the spring of Helicon. A proper
appreciation of the poet's calling pervades the pictures he has
pleasingly coloured; not, perhaps, so richly as faithfully. He
pleases the mind and touches the heart, and no one can read
the poem without pleasure and awarding to the author the poet's
meed."—*Stockton Herald.*

www.ingramcontent.com/pod-product-compliance
Lightning Source LLC
Chambersburg PA
CBHW030625270326
41927CB00007B/1305